Saudi Arabia

Is it possible to ignore the rules of the world – and still enjoy the protection of the international community?

Saudi Arabia does. In Riyadh, a single family is still born into power, having named the country after itself. The king of the family writes the laws, appoints the ministers, selects the judges and pays the clerics.

The dynasty and the nation can thank the outside world for their survival, while maintaining a remarkable distance from international agreements on human and civil rights.

Saudi Arabia is a state that has chosen to remain outside, but is cosseted all the same by governments the world over. A privileged pariah.

The family clings to power with a reference to Islam – while repressing Muslims at the same time.

◆◆◆

Anders Jerichow has listened to people who have seen Saudi prisons from the inside, met the dissident who had to flee and the diplomat who defected. And he has heard numerous others – including Western policymakers – tell their story of the country outside the world of law and order.

Anders Jerichow is Foreign Editor at the Danish daily 'Politiken' and the author of numerous books on the Middle East.

◆◆◆

This is the first in a series of Curzon *Discussion Papers* intended to encourage debate, initially on the subject of religion and politics in the Middle East and in Saudi Arabia in particular.

◆◆◆

By the same author:

Droemmen om Palæstina 1986 (A Dream of Palestine)

Arabiske stemmer 1991 (Arab Voices)

Mellemoestens Hvem Hvad Hvor 1992
(The Who What Where of the Middle East)

Mellemoesten i 90erne 1993 (The Middle East in the Nineties)

Tyrkiet 1995 (Turkey)

Bridging the Cultural Gap 1995

Islam in a Changing World 1996

◆◆◆

Just released:

The Saudi File: People, Power, Politics'

A comprehensive file of documents on Saudi law, human rights, the Massari affair, labour regulations, women, international relations, religious and secular calls for reform and other developments in the Saudi Kingdom.

ISBN 0–7007–0997–5

Saudi Arabia

OUTSIDE GLOBAL
LAW AND ORDER

A Discussion Paper

Anders Jerichow

CURZON

First published in 1997
by Curzon Press
15 The Quadrant, Richmond,
Surrey, TW9 2QA

© 1997 Anders Jerichow

Typeset in New Baskerville by LaserScript, Mitcham, Surrey

Printed in Great Britain by
Biddles Ltd, Guildford and King's Lynn

British Library Cataloguing in Publication Data
A catalogue record for this book is available from the British Library

Library of Congress in Publication Data
A catalogue record for this book has been requested

ISBN 0–7007–0958–4 hbk
ISBN 0–7007–0959–2 pbk

◆◆◆

For Rie

◆◆◆

◆◆◆

I am greatly indebted to Susanne Holst, Politiken, for her continued assistance.

Translations: *Hugh Matthews* and *Patricia Richards Skensved*

Research for this book was made possible by a contribution from Politiken Foundation, Copenhagen

◆◆◆

◆◆◆

'We have nothing to hide.'

King Fahad

in the monarch's first on-line interview
with ArabNet and the daily Okaz, 2 January 1997

◆◆◆

Contents

FOREWORD   xiii

1 ◆ Family Law   1
'As the King deems fit'

2 ◆ Lashed in the School Playground   11
A Day in the Life of Dr Khalifa

3 ◆ Bedouin Society, Industrial Nation   17
'Progress without change'

4 ◆ Justice   27
In the chains of the Muttawas

5 ◆ Independence?   37
No illusions

6 ◆ Social Outcast by Choice   51
Outside international law and order

7 ◆ Protector of the Holy Cities   61
Afraid of Islamists

8 ◆ Women   73
Just half of the population

9 ◆ **Torture**   83
No redress

10 ◆ **Just Allies**   95
Never friends

11 ◆ **'Saudology'**   107
Portrait of a partner

12 ◆ **Massari, refugee in Europe**   115
'A dangerous man'

13 ◆ **Censorship**   127
Operation Desert Shield II

14 ◆ **Harry Wu**   137
Double standards

15 ◆ **Defector in New York**   141
From Diplomat to Refugee

16 ◆ **The Sting**   147
Farewell to the king

CHRONOLOGY   151
BIBLIOGRAPHY   155
ADDRESSES   161
MAPS AND STATISTICS   165

Foreword

A friend?

Saudi Arabia's rulers will not allow this book into the country. It asks a question which in this kingdom is banned: Do Saudis have a claim to the same human rights as people in all other nations? The answer is yes, if you accept the principle of the United Nations' Universal Declaration of Human Rights, the first sentence of which says: 'All people are born free and equal . . .' But in Saudi Arabia the answer is no. One of the world's most powerful autocratic dynasties still rules this secretive kingdom, claiming to be the Protector of Islam's Holy Cities while at the same time keeping its Muslim population in an iron grip.

This book questions the dynasty's birthright to power and its assertion to serve Islam. The book listens to the testimony of some of the victims of the Saud family's repression and several of the courageous individuals who are demanding a reform of the Saudi system.

As a state and a regime, Saudi Arabia enjoys the protection of the West's most powerful governments: the USA, Britain and France. They support Saudi Arabia due to the world's largest known reserves of oil beneath its sands; because the Saud dynasty purchases massive quantities of military hardware; and because they believe that the dynasty vouchsafes stability in the Middle East.

The US, Britain and France know full well that this is a dynasty that represses its own citizens. Nevertheless, they support the Saud regime, in the apparent belief that stability is more important than human freedom, certainly in this particular country for the reasons given above. A US diplomat explains the cynical game: 'There's a difference between an important country and one with which we feel an affinity. Saudi Arabia is important, but we will never sympathize with the values of the Saud family.' Cynicism, though, has its price, paid for by Saudi Arabian citizens when the House of Saud – which calls itself the protector of the Holy Cities of Islam, Mecca and Medina – puts its own survival and power before consideration for its people.

Many of the voices in this book are anonymous. Both Saudis and foreigners who are regular visitors to the kingdom have reason to be cautious; some even to be afraid. Western diplomats in Riyadh refuse to speak openly. They are accustomed to being bugged by the very same royal family their governments in the West protect.

Anders Jerichow

CHAPTER ONE

Family Law

'As the King deems fit'

'Once upon a time there was a king.' That is how a proper fairy tale might begin. Later on, it will be revealed whether the king is good or evil. Good kings usually achieve a lot; evil kings, on the other hand, often suffer a terrible fate – that is, in proper fairy tales.

Real kings can learn something from fairy tales, and as demonstrated by *Ibn Khaldun*, the Arab historian of the 1300s, 'Too much severity harms the monarchy and in most cases will lead to its downfall.'

A king rules in Riyadh. He is a powerful man, so powerful that he allows people to die from the executioner's sword. He dictates the law. He has the right to distribute the wealth of the kingdom, and he can appoint ministers and dismiss them again at will.

This king is so powerful that he alone decides what is good and bad for his country and his subjects. Maybe they love him, honour and respect him for it; maybe not. If not, then they had better keep quiet about it. This king has decided that it is a crime not to approve of him or at least to make one's opinions known to others. For those presumptuous enough to do so, the punishment is prison and a good beating. In fairy tales this sort of thing would lead the culprit to face a sorry end, in this case the king. In Saudi Arabia the king takes his chances.

This is really where the story begins: 'Once upon a time there was a family.' An ancient family, a power-hungry family. For several hundreds of years it endeavoured through force to gain control of the Arabian Peninsula. There were times of glory and times of stagnation since rival families and clans were ever present and the battles were always fought for power and always over the Arabian Peninsula. The year 1902 was a great year since that was when Abdel-Aziz Ibn Saud, the head of the family at that time, won back control of the family's home town, Riyadh, which was the main town in the country of Najd, situated in the heart of the peninsula. So far so good, but there were still other families and the tribal war continued to rage between the Saud family and the rest of the peninsula's most powerful clans. However, in 1932 Abdel-Aziz Ibn Saud had almost realised his secret dream. He had conquered Najd and el-Hasa in the East, Azir in the South and Hejaz with the holy cities of Mecca and Medina in the West, besides more land areas than those already under his own control. What could be a more obvious move than to assemble the kingdom under his own name – and that is precisely what happened.

Saudi Arabia was born, not by popular consensus, not by a democratic election, but by the king's command and sword. Seventy-five years later, the Saud family are still in power and the country is run by sons of Abdel-Aziz Ibn Saud. He must have been a busy man not only in the sphere of war and power politics since at the last count he had 17 wives and 36 sons; the number of daughters is unknown. One of these many wives was a women from the Sudayri clan who bore him seven sons with the right amount of shrewdness and ingenuity to pick up the reins of power after the demise of their father.

This is a very unusual family. In the rest of the world, heads of state are bombarded with popular demands for democracy, for influence in the running of the country, for efficient and honest governments that are answerable to their fellow citizens. In Saudi Arabia, a peoples' demonstration is quickly brought under control. Fahad, one of the Sudayris, dictated his own decree when in 1982 he gave his country the 'basic law', which is not to be confused with a constitution since it is strictly Islam, the Koran and the lore of the prophet that makes up the constitution of Saudi Arabia. This 'basic law' states that the throne must be handed down from Abdel-Aziz Ibn Saud to his sons and from there to his sons' sons. The king chooses his own heir apparent and all government is based in principle on the dictates of the holy Koran and the lore of the prophet.

This is where the problems of both king and country begin. The crux of the matter is power and the legitimisation of power.

It was easier in Ibn Saud's time. His position of power was won after a long and bloody struggle and he believed himself worthy of it. The family had previously allied itself with a hitherto heretic priest, Wahhabi, who gave the name to the orthodox Saudi Wahhabism. At that time there were quite a few rebellions that challenged the ruling interpretations of Islam and right up to the end of the 1920s there were widespread protests in Mecca and Medina against the subjection of the people to the puritanical power of Wahhabism and the Saud family.

Nowadays, the spirit of the age is one of collective responsibility. But this is not the Saud family's style. They are not answerable to anything or anyone but themselves and God and certainly not to their countrymen. Fahad set a precedent when he dictated his basic law and issued his royal decree on the formation of a new advisory council.

'The democratic system that prevails in the world is not suitable for the people who live in our region,' Fahad cheerfully declared in an interview with the Kuwaiti newspaper al-Siyassah. In the monarch's opinion, 'free elections are not in keeping with the structure of Islam'.

◆◆◆

The Saudi Arabian system is the system of the Saud family. Very few words are needed to describe it: The king has the last word. He makes the laws, administrates them and sits in judgement when they are broken. But autocratic rule cannot risk exposing itself on the brink of the year 2000. Fahad has thus introduced an ingenious legal system that controls the interaction between the King, the Council of Ministers, a new Advisory Council ('Majlis al-Shoura') and the relationship with the erudite scholars of Islam. It is an impressive network not least for its efforts to meet both local and international demands to prove its legitimacy. The end result, however, is the same. The King and his family have absolute power. They are born to power; and they retain it by law, their own law that is.

According to the decree, the King is also the head of the Council of Ministers and thus Prime Minister. This post gives him both the legislative and the executive power. Nothing so silly as a segregation of these duties. If the King is absent or disagrees with the rest of the Council, he can veto any opposing decisions. According to the law he is not even obliged to inform the Council of Ministers of his veto.

Thus, the most important decisions are usually restricted to within the confines of the Saud family. Family members are only too pleased to assign themselves

The Saudi System

The King: Appointed by the Royal Family during secret deliberations and powerplay. Controls the ultimate power in the Kingdom, including the right to appoint - and/or dismiss - the Crown Prince.

The Cabinet: A Council of Ministers - selected and appointed by the King and accountable only to the Monarch. In charge of the executive power with Royal Family members in control of key ministries.

Consultative Council: 60 members, all selected and appointed by the King. The consultative (»shoura«) assembly has the right to propose laws and to review - though not the right to change or directly affect - government policies.

Governors: All 14 provinces of Saudia Arabia are headed by a royally appointed governor with a limited local autonomy in economic development. The governors answer directly to the Monarch.

Local Consultative Councils: 10 members in each province, appointed by the local governor and the Minister of Interior. Each consultative council has the right to advice the governor, though not the right to insist on changes in his policies.

the posts of Foreign Minister, Defence Minister and Minister of the Interior.

The King selects – nominates, dismisses and replaces – and this also applies to the new Advisory Council that was finally established in 1992 after several decades of royal assurances. After the Gulf War, in which 30 nations helped to defend Saudi Arabia and free Kuwait, King Fahad must have realized that the time was ripe for a compromise with the modern world in the shape of a move that could be interpreted as a move towards democracy. On that background Saudi Arabia introduced its Advisory Council. This could appear similar to the affairs of state in all other parts of the world, but no one insists on changing anything or on carrying through any new proposals. The decisions of the council have to be presented to the head of the Council of Ministers – also the King – who then presents them to the Council. If it happens that the Council of Ministers and the Advisory Council do not agree, then, as it says in the Royal Decree, Article 17, 'The king decides as he deems fit'.

Saudi Arabia could have developed in a completely different direction. Ibn Saud could have lost his battles or at least some of them. The Arabian Peninsula could have been a collection of several different states and not necessarily one Saudi Arabia. The western Hejaz province could have held its ground, perhaps controlled by the royal family of present-day Jordan since it was from here this family originated. Mecca and Medina could have attained international status for the Muslim world, as was proposed in the 1920s, instead of being under the 'protection' of the Saud family.

It may well be that Fahad did not find free elections suitable in any shape or form but for the Arabian Peninsula they are not a completely new phenomena.

Between 1926 and 1963 regular elections were held to elect the town councils in Hejaz, in the western part of the country. Royal power, however, ended this custom. But, in 1977, the King issued a new law that looked like it would allow for half of the members of the town councils to be freely elected. The royal powers never passed this law. The idea behind it was, however, difficult to eradicate. In December 1990, the demand for local elections was again heard in a dramatic proclamation from Saudi Arabian intellectuals.

The Saud family does have problems with successors to the throne. There are still sons of Abdel-Aziz Ibn Saud to choose from and probably their sons too. But this makes it difficult to ensure that the succession appears legitimate, both in the realm of the family and on an international level. The crux of the matter is that even a family that is born into power is not necessarily immune to dissent within the ranks.

In the early 1960s, a family feud cost King Saud his throne and he was replaced by his brother Faisal. The new basic law gives the king absolute authority – even within the family – to choose a crown prince; this also includes nephews and other male members of the family. However, this does not ensure a definitive solution to the problem of succession on the death of a king and is not one that would impress many scholars of political science in the outside world. A new king still needs the support of the rest of the family. In a game which revolves around absolute power and access to amazing wealth, the stability of the Saud family is constantly threatened by the phenomenal ambitions of the circle of princes – several thousand in all.

The law dictates that the members of this circle are born more worthy of power and status than the rest of the population of Saudi Arabia. This is a very self-assured stand to take, and a very optimistic one. The world has developed in such a way that the constitutions of most nations are built on a degree of democratic control and political responsibility. The Saud family have chosen to rely on the loyalty they demand from their subjects and call it loyalty to the country's culture and to Islam. Either the family is blind or it just refuses to see.

Throughout the Muslim world there is vigorous popular demand for democracy and this even includes the countries of the Persian-Arabian Gulf. In Kuwait, a parliament thrives and even though it has not achieved independence from Emir Sabah, it does allow for a degree of freedom of speech that must frighten the Saud family in Riyadh. These Kuwaiti parliamentarians – the Islamists and the more liberal of them – do not waste words when challenging the Emir family, both light-heartedly and seriously, to take responsibility for their actions in cultural, financial and political matters. In Iran, which while not an Arab country is a Muslim one, the population does not enjoy totally free elections. Nevertheless, other monarchies, including that of Saudi Arabia, looked on in horror when the Iranian people managed to amass enough strength to topple the king, Shah Pahlavi, and introduce a new system which, although it could not be classified as securing total freedom, did allow for a relatively open popular debate. In the 1980s, Saudi Arabia's neighbour, the small country of Bahrain, manifested a powerful opposition to the closure of the parliament which the local monarch Sheikh Khalifa, thought he could abolish at will. In Oman, Sultan Qaboos experimented with allowing some of the members of his advisory committees to be elected locally. South of the kingdom is Yemen, which is slowly moving into a new era, while still with no promise of a new democracy none the less allows a freedom of speech that has never been seen in Saudi Arabia. On the fringes of the Muslim world free elections thrive in the large Muslim nations of Turkey, Pakistan, Bangladesh and to a small extent in Malaysia. Each one of these states has large and lively populations that make Saudi Arabia look like a tiny little nation.

The Saud family must be wondering what on earth is happening. But it is not so difficult to understand. Muslims as well claim the right to say what they think. One after the other Muslim governments have put King Fahad's statements to the test by permitting elections and a political responsibility that he maintains is at odds with Islam. Who is this Saud family that claims it has the sole right to interpret Islam? How does it dare believe in the trust of the nation when it does not even dare ask its citizens the question or accept an answer?

◆◆◆

The Saud family secured its path to control over what later became Saudi Arabia by creating an alliance with the Wahhabi priesthood. Power in modern Saudi Arabia is built on an alliance with the kingdom's Sunni priesthood and on maintaining the holy books as the basis of the kingdom's only rightful constitution.

Despite this, the Saud family does not demonstrate so great a degree of respect for the scribes of Islam that would allow for voluntary and free collaboration. Even though the priesthood and their judges are officially independent, each and every one of them are on the king's payroll. The priests and the 'Council of Senior Ulema' (scholars of the scriptures) are strictly censured just like the rest of the population. They are employed to interpret Islamic law but in all political matters the power of the royal word carries more weight than that of the scholars. Neither has Fahad's basic law given Saudi Arabia an ombudsman nor a court of appeal in those cases where the Council of Ministers, the Advisory Committee and the priesthood conflict with one another. This is not entirely true; as is clearly stated in the statues of the law: the king has the last word. He makes the laws, he administers them and he sits in judgement when they are broken.

CHAPTER TWO

Lashed in the School Playground

A day in the life of Dr Khalifa

Saudi Arabia, 25 May 1995. There was something extraordinary in the air that hot summer morning, but who could know it was to be a display of punishment by lashes? Not Dr Mohamed Kamel Khalifa, a God-fearing Egyptian, who at midday had been dragged out of his dirty cell at the local prison in Bakeereya and driven to the Saoud El Kabir School, where his son used to be in the first grade.

The children were in high spirits, as they usually were expecting something exciting to happen. Several hundred students had been herded into the playground in the little town in the Qasim province and several hundred adults had also crowded in. 'Now it is time for your punishment,' the soldiers said.

Dr Khalifa still remembers the jubilance of the onlookers as the bamboo switch rained down on his back. The children, whipped into a frenzy, shouted abuse, both at him and the Egyptian president Hosni Mubarak. The jubilation increased at every stroke. But between each stroke – there were 80 of them – he also recalled the judge's last words: 'I know you're not guilty, but you must take your punishment.' That day, Mohamed Kamel Khalifa lost his faith in the system of justice in the kingdom of Saudi Arabia.

◆◆◆

He would prefer, in fact, not to tell his story. Dr Mohamed Kamel Khalifa went to Saudi Arabia from Egypt to find peace with his family in the heartland of Islam. Instead, he was to experience a legal system and the kind of injustice he refuses to associate with Islam. Indeed, he would prefer to have peace and quiet for his family, having now found a new job at a local hospital back home in Cairo. Even so, he arrives at a hotel on the banks of the Nile, partly owing Amnesty International his freedom and because he feels obligated to other prisoners in Saudi jails, to tell about the conditions faced by political prisoners. The diminutive, bearded man, accompanied by his *hijab*-clad wife, appear as if from nowhere in the opulent hotel foyer, far from the prison cell into which he had been thrown in defence of his own son.

'I am Dr Mohamed Kamel Khalifa,' he says, 'You know I don't like this?' But the words flow freely from this reserved, mild-mannered gentleman, and just as rapidly from that of his wife. This freedom was not their experience in the court at Bakeereya.

◆◆◆

In mid-June 1994, seven year-old Ahmed came home from school, extremely upset. Although distressed, he was reluctant to tell his parents what had happened in the school attic. It only gradually dawned on the parents, who had now been living in Saudi Arabia for four years, that the school head had enticed the boy into the attic and committed an offence against him.

What was the despondent and angry father to do? He complained to the school. Many weeks and 80 lashes later, Dr Khalifa knew that this was the last thing to have done. First the Muttawa, Saudi Arabia's religious police, turned up and arrested, not the child's alleged abuser, but the father who had complained about the school head. The police urged him to drop his charges. But Dr Khalifa was angry and upset, going straight to the Qasim provincial police, to the local judge and to the province's governor, Prince Faisal bin Bandar al-Saud.

As an Egyptian guest worker – one of the millions of foreigners who have helped to build up and sustain the Saudi Arabian kingdom – Dr Khalifa had now spoken his mind to the entire circle of Saudi Arabia's central power brokers: the prince, a member of the dynasty after whom the nation was named, and which rules absolutely, *inshallah*, with God's help; the local judge, an adminis- trator of Islamic law with a sectarian education, appointed by the ruling Saud dynasty; and the police. Each one had failed the expectations of a man who had moved to Saudi Arabia because, as he said, he felt 'as though I was one of them'.

He wasn't. This much he knew on that autumn day in 1996 when he tells his story. Saudi Arabia, is no pantisocracy. It upholds clear distinctions between members of the Saud dynasty, its subjects and its foreign residents. A month after the incident involving his son, Mohamed Kamel Khalifa was sitting in one of the dynasty's jails, charged with having falsely accused and lied about a school headmaster.

What he did not know – and what should not have made any difference – was that the judge, Abdala El Dakeel and the headmaster were distant relatives, and family ties often provide special connections with the powers that be. It was obvious that the judge was an extremely busy man who had other things to see to. During the five or six court sittings of the trial, when Dr Khalifa was never allowed access to a solicitor, the judge was continuously interrupted and asked to decide on other cases. Nor did Khalifa have anyone from the Egyptian embassy at his side. He only had his son, who stood by his original statement and whom the judge openly accused of lying. The court eventually found Mohamed Kamel Khalifa guilty of lying and defamation of character. The judge then asked the headmaster to leave the courtroom only to tell the condemned man in private: 'I know you're innocent, but you should accept my verdict. Otherwise I shall be forced to send your son to a children's home.'

Dr Khalifa was allowed to leave while the judge decided the terms of his sentence. This was fortunate for both his family and himself. During the few days that followed he managed to get his wife and Ahmed out of the country. Back home in Egypt, the boy was examined by a doctor who was able to confirm that he had been subjected to sexual abuse. While the boy was to receive help – for depression, involuntary urination, anxiety and fits of crying – his father, still in Saudi Arabia, was arrested by soldiers who handcuffed him and dragged him through the streets as a laughing stock. In Cairo, the mother, a courageous and strong-willed woman, contacted the Egyptian Organisation for Human Rights and through them, Amnesty International in London.

Today, Dr Khalifa is convinced that it was Amnesty International's support and coverage of his case by the BBC World Service that secured his freedom after seven days in the local jail and 21 days in the central security prison in El Brida. There he was locked up in a cell with

10 other Egyptians, all of whom had been imprisoned following false accusations by their Saudi 'sponsors' – that is, employers or guarantors who vouch for them during their time in the kingdom.

At this stage, Mohamed Kamel Khalifa still had not lost faith in the higher justice of the realm. He appealed his case, which cost him a nine-month wait without work – his own sponsor deprived him of that. His passport and ID card were still in the keeping of his sponsor as well. But his endeavours were in vain. Dr Khalifa was convicted of slander, receiving a punishment of 80 lashes at the school and 60 lashes outside the mosque on two consecutive Fridays.

In Cairo, his wife knocked on doors, trying to attract the attention of the Saudi Arabian embassy and the Egyptian foreign ministry. At one stage she arranged her own sit-down strike in front of the office of Foreign Minister Amr Moussa on independence square, Al Tahrir, in central Cairo. But she apparently made no impression. More than a million Egyptian guest workers are employed by, and in, Saudi Arabia, but the Egyptian foreign ministry was not keen to fall out with the kingdom.

On 25 May, Dr Khalifa's wife made a phone call to the Egyptian ambassador in Riyadh, who informed her that there was no news. Yet on this very day, Dr Khalifa received his lashings in the school playground in Bakeereya. Children and adults alike hooted and yelled. 'It wasn't the physical pain, he says, but the humiliation and the injustice that hurt.'

Two days later, thanks to the efforts of his wife and international pressure, he went home to Cairo.

The Prince of Qasim, Faisal Bin Bandar al-Saud, a member of the proud, ruling dynasty, did not mince his words: 'Remember,' he said to Dr Khalifa, that the headmaster is the face of our nation. You will not get away with accusing him unpunished.'

The case had nothing whatever to do with Dr Khalifa's son, Ahmed, who had been sexually abused in the school attic. His own back, on the contrary, had been the showground for the kingdom's whip; the display was intended to fill with fear those who were there to hoot and yell on the square.

Since his return, he has been visited by Saudis on several occasions in Cairo. They remind him of the judge's final remark: 'We have a long arm, be careful now, it even reaches as far as your own country.' Dr Khalifa is all too familiar with the strength of that arm: he experienced it in the school yard in Bakeereya.

CHAPTER THREE

Bedouin Society, Industrial Nation

'Progress without change'

To an urban dweller the desert seems silent and inviolable. Sand gets in your eyes when the wind blows; it absorbs moisture at night, and water when it rains, only to return to its dry, inviolable state when the sun comes out again. But as any Bedouin knows the desert is alive and its contours are constantly changing, although it always retains its true identity.

So, too, is Saudi Arabia: a classical Bedouin society in the Arabian desert until the middle of this century, since then the home of hefty economic development which has turned Bedouins into urban dwellers, nomadic herdsmen to modern super-farmers and desert warriors into uniformed soldiers. Nevertheless, they still retain their true identity. This was Saudi Arabia's message when the Ministry of Information in Riyadh inserted advertisements in the international media on 23 September 1992, celebrating '60 years of progress without change'.

Ironically, Saudi Arabia was one of the few countries in the Middle East never to be colonised or to have its borders defined by the imperial powers, because then it was not considered strategically important. Britain and

France and the Ottoman Empire had been extremely busy feathering their nests in countries like Egypt, Syria, the Lebanon, Palestine, Jordan, Iraq and the tribal nations along the Arabian Gulf. On the other side of 'Rub al-Khiali', or the 'empty corner' of the desert, Aden – in what was later to become South Yemen – had long been of strategic importance because of its good harbour on the imperial route to the Southern and Eastern Asia. But the heart of the peninsular was not given much attention by the colonial powers, precisely because of the desert and its remoteness from everything that otherwise tempted hungry empires.

The idea of the world's great powers landing half a million soldiers on the peninsular in 1991/92 to defend this desert and secure the freedom of the little neighbouring emirate of Kuwait would have sounded like a very tall story in the first half of this century.

While the imperial powers competed for the rest of the Middle East, the only ones to be fighting on the Arabian Peninsular were the tribal chiefs. They fought for power over and control of the fulcrum of the Arab tradition in the birthplace of the Prophet in Mecca and the town of Medina, where he founded his Islamic empire and where he was later buried.

One of the tribe or clan leaders, Abdel-Aziz Ibn Saud, who was allied to some of the most orthodox devotees of the puritan Wahhabi sect, had the fortune and the necessary military ingenuity in 1932 to found the enormous kingdom which he named after his own family.

♦♦♦

Saudi Arabia was born and its significance became clear to the international powers in 1937 when the first oil wells showed that the desert concealed incredible wealth in the form of 'black gold'. The vast majority of Saudi Arabia's population were nomadic Bedouins, engaged in trade across the desert and the peninsular or looking after their flocks and small farms, of which only those in mountain regions received enough rain to have any permanence.

The oil was to make such a difference – although only a material one initially – that Saudi Arabia's ruling family and the clergy, who were accustomed to living in isolation from the rest of the world (including the Muslim world) were not interested in opening the country's borders to outside cultural influence.

If that was their ambition, it also became a huge dilemma for Saudi Arabia, especially after oil income started seriously to tempt material change. The clergy found no sympathy for cars, telephones, television or the computers of the modern age. All of it was conceived as inroads by a faithless world outside into the Islamism of the Saud family. But – allegiance with the Wahhabi sect or no – the ruling Saud family was in no mind to miss out on the possibilities the new world had to offer, neither in the form of weaponry to defend borders the Saud family had set, nor in the form of the social development, which the family was now able to buy with its oil money. The result was a compromise, which turned out to be the dilemma of the Saud Wahhabi alliance and the source of its ultimate demise.

Oil revenues, social development and new technology were quickly followed by new forms of education and, unavoidably, by new conceptions of the age and its prospects. From the point of view of the secular royal power it was a question of welfare. From the clergy's point of view, though, it represented a threat to the authoritarian interpretation of Islam and a temptation to be seduced by subversion of the outside world. Their compromise involved the acceptance by the clergy of the entire new social, educational and technological revolution, which was to be implemented 'without change' to the power structure. Saudi Arabia would, like the desert maintain its identity and its inviolability under the uncircumventable banner of Wahhabi Islam.

The material and social development, which was moderate to begin with, became almost explosive in the 1970s. The old Bedouin community which accounted for the majority of the population two decades earlier, had been reduced to just 10 per cent by the late 1970s.

The influx to the towns was enormous – two-thirds of the population were suddenly urban – with all that entails in terms of the demand for new housing, new industries and jobs, schools and health services. Only the explosion in the international price of oil in the wake of the Israeli-Arab October war in 1973 enabled Saudi Arabia's rulers to avoid serious dislocation.

It was not that there was a lack of things to be done. Roads, housing, schools and hospitals were built and a public administrations and private companies were established. But Saudi Arabia's own citizens were only prepared to enjoy the fruits of development, not work towards it, as they were not yet trained to do the jobs that needed to be done. Instead, millions of foreign workers and experts were imported; unskilled workers from Southern Asia and the Far East, middle-ranking technicians from other Arab countries in the Middle East and fully-trained so-called 'experts' from the West.

Instead of waiting for Saudi workers to complete their training, the royal family in Riyadh used its new oil billions to guarantee both training and occupations for their own citizens. All children attended school and young people were offered higher education. Young

Saudi couples were given economic assistance to set up home. Health care was free and local transport prices kept low with enormous subsidies. Everything money could buy was bought in the 1970s: new roads, new weaponry, new palaces for the royal family, new oil installations – even farms were transplanted into an environment where before they would have been mirages.

The new establishments were most striking when seen from the air. Right in the middle of the desert, the circular fields appeared as if from nowhere, sometimes almost shockingly green in contrast to the surrounding desert yellow sand. It seemed like a revolution, and in a sense it probably was; Saudi Arabia was suddenly producing its own tomatoes and its own wheat in enormous quantities. But it was a costly revolution in more than one sense. Most of these artificially irrigated farms in the desert were manned by Asian guest workers, while their owners sat in the shade. The farms even with huge state subsidies, could only operate successfully with massive quantities of water. This water was either in the form of expensively desalinated sea water, or what was environmentally even more costly, from tapping the nation's fresh water reserve beneath the desert sands. These water layers were suddenly and drastically depleted when the new farms came into being in places where nature had never intended them to be.

The dilemma of the power-policy compromise was not something that could simply be cast off. Saudi Arabia's new educational system did not exactly live up to international standards of creativity and critical thinking. Instead, it stuck to tradition with the emphasis on learning by role and respect for prevailing authority. All the same, the new learning did create new demands for more information and material change.

Although the country's boundaries were still closed to tourism and to free entry and departure, the Saud family had invited so many guest workers and 'experts' into the country that every third individual in the kingdom was a foreigner. They had no ties with either the traditions of Saudi Arabia or Wahhabi interpretations of Islam. Both from within and without, the seeds had been sown of demands or expectations of other ways of life than that based on established Bedouin tradition.

Although the Saud dynasty had promised the clerics that they would maintain the nation's moral codex and keep the amorality of the West at bay, the leaders of the Saud dynasty were well acquainted with other ways of living than in the shadow of the mosque and the renunciation of earthly pleasures. The younger generation of the dynasty were sent in large numbers to the USA and Britain to get the best education.

During the first decade after the oil boom in 1973–74, developments led to some coarse-grained contrasts: huge numbers of effectively unemployed, state-subsidised Saudi Arabians living side by side with underpaid guest workers. Increasing numbers of fully-trained Saudi Arabians without the prospect of employment in a free labour market. Ever-improving levels of social welfare without its consumers either paying for it or fixing its price.

Most of the oil from the world's largest reserves was sent directly to refineries abroad, rather than Saudi Arabia making use of the potential of full employment in oil production. In the meantime, inflation skyrocketed. The public administration employed hoards of Saudi Arabians without demanding anything of them or expecting to show anything for the salary they were paid.

Deep inside Saudi Arabia this was interpreted by some as an attempt to 'corrupt' the society. Saudi Arabia certainly avoided the slums, unemployment and social frustrations that followed in the wake of rapid urbanisation in countries such as Turkey and numerous Latin American societies in the 1960s, 1970s and 1980s.

Abroad, Saudi Arabia did not seem to have changed. The men still proudly wore their ankle-length coats and the women their top-to-toe black gowns with only a net in front of the face. But behind the facade and the proud traditions, the same Saudi Arabians had been confronted with international competition in their new education system and a new bombardment of information from the world outside. Moreover, the Saudis had to decide exactly what it was they wanted of their welfare society, which a hereditary royal power had financed, built and corrupted.

This decision have been delayed by a few more years had the oil pumps only been allowed to work undisturbed. The Saud family had admittedly done what it could to distribute its work-free sources of growing wealth. In other countries, the same system would have been considered corrupt. In Saudi Arabia, however, it became an efficient industry for local Saudis to take a 'commission' for acting as a middleman (it required no work on their part) between foreign companies and Saudi Arabia. As early as 1977 it was decided that no Saudi should, officially, represent more than 10 foreign companies. This distributed work-free incomes which, until then, had made members of the royal family especially immensely rich.

But although they were legal in Saudi Arabia, these incomes still tended to be centred largely on today's 5,000 princes and other families with 'access' to those who really hold the power. Equally naturally, the 'commission' system gave rise to both religious and secular criticism of growing corruption in the kingdom.

At the same time, Saudi Arabia was burdened by two Gulf wars. In the first of these – between Iraq and non-Arab Iran from 1980–88 – the Saud family, out of self-interest, helped the Iraqis with both gifts and loans that were never repaid.

The other Gulf war – following Iraq's invasion of Kuwait in 1990–91 – cost Saudi Arabia almost half its financial reserves. It paid the lion's share of having half a million soldiers in the kingdom and the campaign to liberate Kuwait in January and February 1991.

The Saudi Arabia economy was in dire straits and to make matters worse, the war had not forced oil prices up. Saudi Arabia's national income had experienced a drastic fall and the Riyadh government was faced with an unpleasant, unaccustomed budget deficit.

Despite heavy investment in local industry and attempts to spread the nation's income base, oil was in the mid-1990s still the source of three-quarters of the Saudi Arabian government's income. Oil also accounted for more than three quarters of exports from the kingdom. Drastic measures were decreed by the king in the next five-year plan: the deficit had to go. More Saudi Arabians would have to work, that is, do proper, productive work, with the desired consequence that foreign workers would be sent home and state subsidies to water and electricity and domestic food production would be cut back.

This move was no different than any other government would have made in a similar situation, but Saudi Arabia in not any country. Its population has to a great extent not been accustomed to working for its income, not used to paying cost price for food, water and electricity. Until now, the country's gifts had been seen as rewards for the power the dynasty had reserved for itself. The demand that Saudi Arabians should take over more productive work might act like a boomerang against the ruling dynasty. In other countries it has always been natural for the imposition of taxes to be followed up by demands from those who pay it. Of course, in Saudi Arabia the rulers have been financed more by oil income than taxation. But the oil, too, is public, common property. It is written in the law that the oil belongs to the nation and not the Saud dynasty. And if the dynasty starts making demands on its subjects, they may very well start making demands the other way. This will make it extremely difficult for the powers that be to insist on progress without change.

CHAPTER FOUR

Justice

In the chains of the Muttawas

The home in Saudi Arabia is a safe place: it is even written into the law. Within the home, the woman can cast aside her veil, leaving the family by itself. No police, no Muttawa – the kingdom's religious law and order corps – are allowed to invade people's privacy. At least, that is what Patrick and Nerie Foster thought. But they were wrong.

One evening in 1992, 18 months after the USA, England and 28 other nations had ensured the safety of Saudi Arabia and liberated Kuwait, there was a knocking at the gate. Nerie was alone with their children, Christina, aged four, Maria, who was two, and Patrick junior, one. Nerie Foster, a Filipino Catholic married to an Englishman, was scared. Earlier that evening, one of the family's Filipino visitors had left to get cigarettes but had not returned. An English friend had taken the same stroll to the kiosk on the corner to look for him, but did not return either. Patrick Foster, Nerie's husband, an insurance agent who had been head-hunted for Saudi Arabia a year before, decided to go to the kiosk to look for his friends and buy the cigarettes. 'Back in a minute,' he said.

It took ten and a half months for him to return. He had just bought the cigarettes when a hand grabbed hold of him and heaved him out of the shop. Two Muttawas knocked him to the ground, handcuffed and fettered him and threw him into a car with blood streaming down his face.

Nerie knew nothing about this, but sensed a sudden fear. Two friends and her husband had disappeared. She took the children upstairs to the bedroom, uneasy but aware that she could not do anything herself that evening. To leave on her own was out of the question. As a woman she was not allowed to go about unaccompanied, driving a car was equally an illegal action. And she could not leave the children.

At about 2 a.m. she heard a noise outside. Someone was hammering on the gate. The street was lit by the headlights of a car. Nerie peeped out from upstairs but kept away from the door. She could see two Muttawas climbing over the fence – simultaneously breaching Muslim tradition and breaking Saudi Arabian law. Now they were hammering at the door. In a minute they had broken the door, these bearded orthodox civil guards, whose job it was to protect Islam and moral virtue in the Saudi kingdom.

Nerie waited for almost 20 minutes before she opened the bedroom door. She had expected the Muttawas to burst in when the children started to cry. But her night-clothes kept them at a distance. 'Put on your *abbaya*,' the Muttawas shouted, throwing in one of the black, ankle-length garments to make her cover herself up.

Shortly afterwards she heard the sound of fetters in the hall. She just managed to catch a glimpse of another pair of Muttawas with Patrick between them before she was pulled aside.

◆◆◆

Half a night earlier. In the Muttawas' car, Patrick Foster felt the blood running down his cheeks. At their 'station' they asked him to clean his face. 'Not before the British embassy has got a picture of what I look like now,' shouted Foster, as though he did not realise that it still could get much worse. For some reason, the Muttawas threw him into their car, taking him to the local casualty department, where an Indian doctor and a Filipino nurse sewed up the gash in one of his eyelids with four stitches and repaired the brow above the other eye with two. Then he went back to the Muttawa station in handcuffs and rattling fetters. He could forget all about the British embassy. The Muttawas, moreover, felt no obligation to present any charges.

Patrick Foster cursed the whole situation. He could have been out of Saudi Arabia now; ought to have been. The Saudi government had found him in England in late 1990 and offered him an easy, well-paid job at a medical insurance company, initially for two years. He arrived in December 1990, five months after Iraq had invaded Kuwait and while the USA was in full swing landing troops to defend Saudi Arabia and later to liberate Kuwait. This perhaps was not the most promising time to arrive in the Middle East, but Foster had arrived to earn some money for his family's future. That was not how it was meant to be. But Foster made the mistake of criticising a Saudi colleague. And twenty months into his contract, he was told bluntly that his services were no longer required. If only he had just returned to Nerie and the children. But Foster still wanted to go to Kouba south of Riyadh to say goodbye to some friends. He rented a brand new Mercedes 230 with fully comprehensive insurance. Unfortunately, he was involved in an accident with a Saudi car, in which the passenger, an elderly Saudi women, died.

'Don't worry; it was the will of Allah', said the old widower, when meeting face to face a week later at a police station. Foster declared his willingness to pay a *diyya'* – blood money – in compensation. The car's insurance company would be ready to put the *diyya* on the table. But the Saudi was adamant that he didn't want any money and they parted. The firm Patrick Foster had just left, however, was not satisfied. They insisted on having the old man's signature or finger print on a declaration stating that he did not want a *diyya*. However, neither Foster nor the police had the man's name or address. The firm refused to return the Foster family's passports until the matter had been cleared up.

Without his passport, Foster was unable to get new work in the kingdom. From being headhunted to Riyadh, he now felt like a hostage, consuming the savings he was supposed to have brought to England. Until then, Foster had been a law-abiding man, apart from a few drinks within the four walls of his own home. He hardly figured that as a crime. He would know better. But caught in a trap, Patrick Foster began selling alcohol. Perhaps he found it a form of insurance that among his customers for alcohol he had the highest ranking Saudi executive of the firm that brought him to the country. When they dragged him into his own home in handcuffs and fetters, Foster's first concern had not been the store of alcohol hidden under the stairs. He could not help noticing how easily the Muttawas simply invaded a private home. But what really overwhelmed him was the experience of finding his home totally empty. No Nerie, no children. That they were being held in a room upstairs he did not realise until several weeks later.

The Muttawas obviously had no scruples once they had started ransacking the house. They found the drink very quickly. Foster admitted his responsibility without further ceremony. They also made him open Nerie's jewellery case, the contents of which one of the Muttawa's simply tipped into his pocket. But when they presented him with a little lump of hashish, Foster denied all knowledge of it with a horrible feeling of having been set up. Patrick Foster had never been involved with hash. After the Muttawas had thrown him into a car, and while Nerie looked on, they emptied the house of the video, the radio, the stereo and the fax machine, while they cursed the pig meat that was revealed in the freezer.

◆◆◆

Patrick Foster says he had never seen an uncivilised place as the cell at the police station they threw him into. In this facility he met the two friends who earlier that evening had disappeared on their way to buy cigarettes, together with over 20 others, in a filthy basement cell. The lavatory was a hole in the floor in a little cubicle; no paper, no soap. Nor were there beds or mattresses, just the bare floor for the nights sleep. In the corridor the 'dog-kennels' could be seen, cells so small that prisoners had to sit hunched up. The light remained on, day and night.

No charges were made. There was no possibility of calling the British embassy, and no lawyer was present. Worst of all, Patrick Foster still had no idea what had happened to his wife and children.

Nerie too, was bundled, together with the children, into one of the Muttawas' cars and driven off to a women's jail to share a cell with over 20 other prisoners. A few of them had bunks, but Nerie and the children had to sleep on the floor.

They spent three weeks like this. Nerie denied every-thing, for safety's sake, including the alcohol in the house. In the meantime she witnessed a kind of human degradation she had never imagined. One of the other prisoners in her cell was a young woman from Sri Lanka who had been brought in to give birth to her baby. Like so many other imported home assistants and child minders, she had been raped by her Saudi sponsor – who has his employee's passport and future in the palm of his hand – but he would not admit to having made the girl pregnant. His disdainful Saudi wife had her thrown into jail, where she had just given birth when Nerie arrived.

But the Sri Lankan was also to be subjected to corporal punishment: 900 lashes with rubber piping. When they brought her back down – she got about 70 lashes at a time – the other women were allowed to put ice on her lacerated back. After the last lashes had been administered the woman was to be deported, but Saudi Arabia would keep her little girl. The women in that overfilled cell did not dare to think what kind of future the child would be offered.

Eventually, Nerie and the children were deported, not to their home in England but, because of Nerie's passport, to the Philippines.

♦♦♦

In Patrick Foster's prison there was no ice. When a prisoner had been subjected to the rubber pipe they rubbed toothpaste into their backs, which had a cooling effect.

Foster first had to pass through the drug squad prison, where he was immobilised with handcuffs and fetters made in the UK, although their use there is illegal. At the drug squad establishment he was ordered into a large hall, where the first 150 male prisoners sat or stood for 20 hours out of 24 with their faces to the wall. The prisoners who complained or even murmured were suspended by their wrists with their arms spread like a cross with their feet hanging loose. Once in a while they were subjected to a round of *falakka* – painful lashings to the soles of the feet.

The chief interrogator wanted Foster's signature on an admission of possession of hashish. Foster refused, pointing out that he had admitted having alcohol but that the hashish must have been put there by the Muttawas. 'You shouldn't say that to the judge, he's a Muttawa himself,' the chief interrogator said. 'Then you'll really be in trouble.'

After five days Foster was returned to the ordinary jail and from there to the Malaz jail in Riyadh, a 'diabolical pig-sty' as Foster puts it. His bed was the bare floor. The walls were lattice-work that let in the ferocious heat during the day. The desert cold came in the same way by night, as did the sand-storms and rain, since Riyadh's winter was setting in. There was no means of keeping clean.

Foster secretly took notes of what he had experienced, 'Just to save myself from going mad.' Almost every day the prisoners were forced to see and hear fellow inmates being lashed and beaten. On numerous Fridays, prisoners who had been convicted of theft were picked up to be taken to the 'Chop-chop square', where people thronged to after prayers. Two military policemen held the prisoner by one shoulder. A thong was bound tightly round the opposite upper arm, while two more policemen took hold of another thong which was bound tightly round the two middle fingers on the hand of that arm. Then it was the executioner's turn. Foster had thought that they took off the hand in one dramatic chop. Not so, a Sudanese told him after the event. The executioner first slowly cut an oversized 'v' into both surfaces of the hand pulling the skin back. Then a the big knife separated the hand from the arm. This was followed by a trip to the hospital to have the skin flaps sewn together. All was carried out without anaesthetic.

Patrick Foster managed to teach three fellow prisoners to write with their left hand. Once in a while they would push their stump of a right arm against the floor in an attempt to defy the pain.

Yet another cell-mate was collected one Friday. He did not return. Before they came for him he gave Foster a letter to his family. It was a terrifying day, for Foster as well: his cell-mate had been convicted of producing alcohol, as had he.

◆◆◆

Every day, Foster took notes and crossed off the days on a piece of paper he bought from fellow prisoners, studying Islam to get their sentences reduced; they were halved if the prisoners converted. Foster was able to use their paper to write a several hundred-page diary, which he successfully had smuggled out piece by piece and sent to England.

One day, like all the other prisoners, he was handcuffed and fettered and finally placed before his judge. Foster admitted to being guilty of distributing alcohol, but denied having produced it – he quite simply did not possess the necessary equipment. The entire case was in Arabic, without an interpreter, without a defence lawyer and without the defendant given the right to say anything further. The court found Foster guilty. The punishment: six months imprisonment for liquor distribution, 10 months for producing it plus 200 lashes followed by deportation.

Not quite a month later a visitor turned up from the British embassy who was able to inform him that he had been given a further five months for possession of hash. Foster had never faced a court on that count. In all, he could now expect 21 months behind bars plus the lashes and deportation. When King Fahad granted him amnesty after 10 months Foster says, 'I was just about to say "No thank-you" – after all, how could I accept a pardon for a crime I hadn't committed? But then I reconsidered.'

Foster was free before he had needed toothpaste to relieve the pain in his back. It was now 6 September 1993, but he still was not free to leave the country. His old Saudi employers insisted on the matter of the traffic accident and the blood money being sorted out. The old widower had reappeared. He planned to remarry and now needed the money. But the insurance claim was by now out of date.

Foster did manage to obtain the money. The most friendly of the officers at the police station let him have some time in the more lenient traffic police prison giving him a chance to ask his mother in England to send him the blood money.

Finally, the sponsor who had brought Patrick Foster to Saudi Arabia in the first place, was prepared to give him back his passport. The prison officer invited Foster to a farewell dinner. After the ample meal the officer sent his wife and children out of the room and opened a cupboard. Would Foster like to join him in a cognac?

The following day, a Tuesday, an elated Foster was able to call the British embassy to inform them that he was a free man and wanted to fly British Airways to Heathrow on the Thursday. 'Marvellous,' the consul replied. 'So you can just manage to join us on Wednesday. We're having a cocktail party.'

CHAPTER FIVE

Independence?

No illusions

Abdullah bin Abdul-Aziz bin Muammar arrived in Rome with a message: 'Look after your own affairs', said the prince. The occasion was the United Nations Summit on Food Security. It was 15 November 1996, a dramatic day for international collaboration. As far as it goes the reason for the meeting was simple. While some people in the world constantly fight the problem of being overweight, others still suffer from hunger. In Rome the aim was to demand solidarity from the nations of the world.

The low attendance at the meeting was not a promising sign. More than a few heads of state and government leaders stayed at home. This was true of Fahad of Saudi Arabia and his crown prince, but, Abdullah bin Abdul-Aziz bin Muammar, the Minister of Water and Agriculture did attend.

> 'It is not an optimal situation', he was quoted as saying in the *Egyptian Gazette*, that 'underdeveloped countries are, to a large extent, dependent on emergency food supplies from affluent countries and international organisations.'

'These underdeveloped countries', he went on, 'must be prepared to take the problem of unstable food supplies more seriously. They must approach the issue with more realism, decisiveness and independence on the basis of their own resources, potential and population.'

These were bold words. The agricultural minister was not alone in calling on the poor nations of the world to work harder at standing on their own feet. But his country is hardly the best example of a nation that has solved its problems without indebting itself to the international community.

The day Iraqi tanks rolled into Kuwait, 2 August 1990, the Royal Family of Saudi Arabia did not dare trust its own 'resources, potential and people' for more than a few hours before it called on the USA for protection – a plea for help which the USA was more than willing to answer. For the majority of the population of Saudi Arabia this move came as a considerable shock. Ever since the beginning of the 1970s, the Saud family had invested enormous amounts of money in increasing the strength of the country's military defence system. It had spent billions of Riyals on new military bases, modern tanks, jet aircraft and even middle-distance rocket missiles; the last were provided by China which caused outrage in the USA, while the rest were mostly provided by the USA, Britain and France. The process of rearmament occurred to the accompaniment of royal rhetoric on the will and the ability of the country to protect itself from attack.

On 2 August 1990, the illusory bubble burst. Up until this point the royal powers – 'the protectors of Islam's two holy cities, Mecca and Medina' – had done everything in their power to keep foreign influence down to a minimum. Without a moment's hesitation they were now inviting godless US soldiers – including women – to cross the borders of Saudi Arabia in order to help defend Islam and the country's 'independence'.

Immediately after the war, Saudi Arabian women could be arrested for demanding the right to drive a car during a demonstration in Riyadh. In contrast, to save their own skins, the Saud family had allowed tough US females to race through the streets of Dhahran in military vehicles. It was the USA's decision not to discriminate against female soldiers just because it happened to be Saudi Arabia the troops were being sent to.

However, such political correctness on the part of the Saud family during the war was not evident in other areas. From his recollections of the war the US Minister of Defence, Colin Powell, was able to tell us of the Saud family's unwillingness to allow Christian and Jewish services to be conducted in the kingdom. At the same time it was perfectly acceptable – with the consent of the USA and the Saud family themselves – to allow young Christian and Jewish Americans to risk their lives for the sake of the kingdom. Prince Bandar was willing to allow tens of thousands of body bags to be sent to Saudi Arabia in expectation of great losses – but 'no bibles'. The American defence ministry had in fact received a large number of bibles from religious groups in the USA. Powell could just imagine the kind of response he would get if the military tried to tell these people that Saudi Arabia would gladly take their sons but not the bibles. Prince Bander insisted: 'The Saudi customs officers are under an obligation to confiscate bibles.' Eventually, a compromise was reached in which the bibles were flown directly to US air bases where Saudi officials would turn a blind eye. But no Jewish services must be conducted on Saudi land, Bandar said. 'They can die defending your country but they must not pray in it?', asked Powell. Bandar was adamant: he was afraid that his people would see on television Jewish prayer meetings being held in their country. Finally, it was agreed that the USA would fly its Jewish soldiers from the mainland to US ships in the Gulf where they could conduct their services. At the same time Powell was forced to promise that US soldiers would not walk the streets wearing crucifixes and that they would otherwise be ordered to wear their crucifix inside and not outside their shirts.

These requirements were degrading for the US military who were putting young American lives at Saudi Arabia's disposal. But it was not all easy for the royal family either, having boasted for years of their position as the protectors of the two holy cities, Mecca and Medina. The illusion of ultimate independence was a balloon that burst during the Gulf War, but if the truth be known the dynasty of Saudi Arabia has actually never been able to maintain autonomy.

For decades there has been a foreign worker or a body of experts for every third inhabitant in Saudi Arabia. These foreigners have gradually made themselves indispensable and it is a fact that they have contributed the most to the modernization of the kingdom. Right from the start migrant workers founded the oil fields, laid down pipelines from Dammam to Jubail and in some places built over-sized motorways. They have built schools and cleaned the streets. Other migrant workers – doctors and nurses – have staffed the new hospitals and yet others have built power stations, water purification plants and controlled the desalination of sea water. There is a very long list of projects and tasks that Saudi Arabians were not willing – or not able – to carry out themselves.

Revenue from the oil industry had made it possible to buy everything that was needed including migrant workers from the East, experts from the West, new technology and weapons; in this way the Saud family thought they could buy security. But when the day of judgement arrived on 2 August 1990, all this hardware was of no value as long as the Saud family remained unable to 'look after their own affairs'. This was a humiliating experience for the Saud family and their exposure was exploited by the growing opposition. During the war the opposition was responsible for a steady distribution of illegal cassettes carrying recorded protests against the royal family's decision to place the independence of the kingdom into the hands of godless foreigners. Questions were also raised as to why such huge investments were unable to help Saudi Arabia to defend itself.

At the United Nations meeting the Minister of Agriculture, Abdullah bin Abdul-Aziz bin Muammar, inadvertently took the matter of one of Saudi Arabia's essential problems to the extreme: does any country look after its own affairs in the 1990s?

At the summit meeting in Rome the keywords were 'food security', or in other words a country's capacity for providing enough food for its population. This had been one of Saudi Arabia's own ambitions: self-sufficiency in food. When the vast areas of desert that dominate the Arabian Peninsula are taken into account, this was a formidable objective. However, in the 1980s government subsidies turned this mirage into reality. The wheat on the gigantic farms stood proud and tall, not so much the result of any rain dance but more the product of ridiculously expensive government subsidies. In fact, Saudi Arabia – of all countries – achieved far beyond what was required for food security in respect of grain. A countries of desert and oil became a main exporter of wheat, in spite of the desert and thanks to the oil industry. Production reached its height in 1991/92 with a harvest of 4.1 million tons which was much more than the 1.7 million tons needed by the country. This was a magnificent demonstration of the power of money. If the irrigation had suddenly stopped or the flow of subsidies had slowed, the wheat would have withered in next to no time.

This is precisely what happened. Money cannot buy everything. As early as 1992 the government of Riyadh began to impose restrictions on the government subsidies for Saudi Arabian farmers. Production fell at such a rapid rate that by 1996/97, faced with a predicted production of 1.3 million tons, Saudi Arabia was again preparing to import corn. Towards the end of the 1980s Riyadh would have considered it a risk to depend on foreign production in this way. In the 1990s, it is a necessary evil.

When Saudi Arabia gave up paying for 'independence', it was also due to the realisation that 'food security' was not dependent on where the wheat was produced but also a question of market supply. The money Riyadh had spent over decades, trying to maintain an absurdly expensive production of wheat in one of the world's hottest and driest countries, could without a doubt have secured the purchase on the international market of far more wheat from healthier agricultural areas.

The Gulf War precipitated another burning issue. Who was actually dependent on whom – the West on Saudi Arabia with its huge, easily accessible supplies of oil or the opposite? For the Saud regime it was comforting to experience how quickly and willingly 30 nations rose to defend Saudi Arabia and liberate Kuwait. A Western diplomat has stated that 'the collapse of Saudi Arabia is the worst scenario the West can imagine in the Middle East'.

The Saud family would undoubtedly not like to hear the different observations now being made in those Western capitals that contributed to the defence of Saudi Arabia.

'We once thought our dependence on Saudi oil did not allow us the freedom to choose', says a government official with a central position in the US State Department; he is one of the diplomats involved in defining American policy on the Arabian Peninsula. 'They are still the most accessible and the largest reserves of oil we know of and this situation will continue for at least another decade. However, other oil-producing countries are beginning to make their presence felt, amongst these are those of Central Asia. Furthermore, the Gulf War has shown us that the government of Riyadh is essentially dependent on us for its military security. This alters the balance of power .'

In London, a Middle East expert in Whitehall has turned his attention to two other factors. One is that 20 years after the first 'oil crisis', the price of oil is more or less back to the same level as before that crisis. This clearly demonstrates that the oil market tends towards stability. Even the last Gulf War did not create an extended period of alarmingly high prices. The other factor, the expert says, is that

'it is clear that the Saud regime seems to be very busy settling differences with other sources of potential instability. After decades of not acknowledging its borders with neighbouring countries, Riyadh has now agreed to a border settlement with Oman and hopes to negotiate the same kind of treaty with its more difficult neighbours, Yemen and Qatar. It has also abolished its support of certain destabilizing forces in Egypt and despite the PLO's support of Iraq during the Gulf War, has now resumed negotiations with the chairman of the PLO Yasser Arafat. In my estimation the Saud regime wants peace and stability outside the country in order to concentrate on internal problems.'

Not very far away in another part of London, the Saudi religious leader-in-exile Professor Massari expresses another opinion on the Saudi Arabian issue, one which the royal power in Riyadh hates and fears.

'Oil supplies are not the prerogative of the Saud regime. A new system in Saudi Arabia would also export oil, if only for their own sake.'

The Whitehall source says:

'It is difficult to imagine any ruling powers in Saudi Arabia not having the maintenance of oil production as their first priority. After all, it is all the country has. It is much the same situation in Iran. Not even Ayatollah Khomeini, probably the most anti-Western ruler in the Middle East, would cut oil supplies to Western capitals.'

The worst scenario imaginable: 'A total collapse'. The western diplomat reiterates his nightmare during a meeting in a European capital. He is reluctant to go into too many details but nevertheless makes it clear that as far as the rest of the world is concerned the worst outcome must be a breakdown in oil production. This is 'difficult to imagine', says a source in the British government's political research unit.

'Such a move would presuppose an internal civil war which would destroy oil production, bring related industries to a halt and after a while eat away at the economic foundations of Saudi Arabian society itself. Masseri is therefore right when he says that it would be in the interests of any new power to start the oil pumps up again as quickly as possible. And there is no place on earth where oil is so easily accessible as in Saudi Arabia. Even after the most devastating crisis, oil production could be resumed very quickly. Kuwait is an excellent example of how quickly a recovery can be made when we recall the images of burning oil fields and mass destruction that characterized the end of the war.'

However, it is very difficult – if not to say impossible – to get policy-makers in London or Washington to reflect on other scenarios of a peaceful or rapid revolution in Riyadh. Western policy is based solely on the notion that the Saud dynasty will either exist forever – 'this is not very likely', says an American diplomat who has been in office in several Middle Eastern capitals – or that it will voluntarily relinquish its power. 'This is not very likely either', the diplomat adds dryly. But Saudi Arabia has learnt at least one thing from the events of the 1990s: as far as the rest of the world is concerned it can no longer bank on independence, whether it is a matter of wheat, oil or military security.

The fact that oil production is increasing on an international level, combined with the oil countries' inability to come to any price agreement has made a significant rise in price levels impossible. It is therefore highly inexpedient to cultivate one's own wheat at sky high prices. Indeed, why cultivate expensive wheat when one can otherwise buy it cheaply? In the name of independence or self-sufficiency? This can only be an option if something prevents you from buying wheat on the international market – a highly unlikely development.

Saudi Arabia has the oil, but the international community determines the conditions. Neither the country itself nor the circle of oil-producing countries in OPEC can dictate a price any longer.

Up until the Gulf War the Saud family thought that oil was enough to ensure military security. It could indeed pay for the purchase of the world's best weapons, but as it turned out, this was not enough and the country was forced to request support from outside. Help did arrive, but Saudi Arabia will not be able to foot the bill of many more conflicts of this kind.

◆◆◆

Since the war, gigantic imports of weapons reveal that Riyadh is unsure as to whether the rest of the world will keep the military forces of Iraq at bay. Neither does it trust the other great power in the Gulf, Iran.

The country's financial problems since the war has also put all Saudi Arabia's expectations of total independence to shame; when all is said and done, the royal power has made Saudi Arabia dependent on the West for its security. The kind of society that has developed in the kingdom similarly relies on manpower from poorer countries.

This kind of dependence is something Saudi Arabia and the reigning dynasty cannot afford, but which it may have tremendous difficulty avoiding. For two decades, a third of the kingdom's population – some 18 million – consisted of guest workers from overseas, most of them unskilled Asians, who carried out the laborious construction work beneath the merciless Arabian sun. Others filled a wide variety of service jobs, together with many 'experts' from the West and the rest of the Middle East.

Although their services were relatively cheap, they have still cost money – while other money was used to pay Saudis not to do anything in particular.

Now, at least officially, guest workers in an increasing number of jobs are to be replaced by Saudi Arabians. That will not be easy to achieve. It could require a cultural revolution just to get a Saudi Arabian into the hot sun with a shovel, now that they have got used to foreigners doing anything for money. Moreover, Saudi Arabians expect much higher salaries than what they paid foreigners. Attempts will be made all the same as part of the 'Saudi-isation' programme'. In 1994/5, the number of migrant workers from Egypt was reduced from 1.2 million to 900,000. Everything in Saudi Arabia is strictly controlled and the granting of work permits is no exception to the rule. The authorities have clamped down on the 'importing' of certain types of job, for instance it is now forbidden to 'import' secretaries. Each and every business in Saudi Arabia has been issued with instructions to increase the number of nationals on the pay roll by 5 per cent per annum.

There are other ways to describe the inability to rely on 'own resources, own potential and own population'. Despite the enormous investments in Saudi Arabian hospitals, Saudi princes do not hesitate to make – albeit clandestine – use of the treatments offered by the Israeli Hadassah hospital in Jerusalem and another in Haifa. When the king falls ill nothing can reassure the court more than a US specialist. Some would call it international 'co-operation' and both the Israeli and the US doctors seem happy to be of service. However, when the country's professed aim has always been to look after itself and avoid dependence on others, this practice is an expression of abject failure especially if one takes into account the decades of extremely expensive measures taken to promote development.

Money will never again be so plentiful as it was at the time when OPEC had relative control over oil prices. Riyadh has every good reason to fear that the international community's willingness to help at the beginning of the 1990s might now be followed by international expectations – even demands – for democracy in the country.

This is not the Saud dynasty's plan. The Gulf War became a symbol of the old world's hope of the beginning of a new era. In Washington President Bush talked about a 'new world order' based on the united front of honest governments against the 'evil regime' led by Saddam Hussein in Iraq. And in the Gulf, the hope of a new sense of international responsibility was born from the strength shown by the 30 countries who rose to defend Saudi Arabia against the threat from Iraq – and ensured the liberation of Kuwait.

In honour of the end of the Cold War, an international understanding was established during the Gulf War between the East and the West. Nevertheless, 'Operation Desert Storm' did conceal intransigent internal differences. The freedom alliance included quite a few repressive regimes: Saudi Arabia itself, but other Arab powers in the Gulf as well. These included a few that had troops stationed on foreign soil – Syria (controlling most of Lebanon) and Morocco (occupying most of Western Sahara) – and others that were far from ready to introduce anything resembling a democratic system.

Despite this, the liberation of Kuwait was a sign that the world was ready for change and was preparing to move into a new era. If any countries were in debt to the new dreams it was the freedom alliance's two victors. In Kuwait and Saudi Arabia, two family regimes owed their survival to the rest of the world. Their dependence was documented. However, from the Saud family's point of view this did not necessarily mean that Saudi Arabia was bound to adopt the political system of democracy.

CHAPTER SIX

Social Outcast by Choice

Outside international law and order

Even before the Gulf War there were signs of the world beginning to pull itself together. The Berlin Wall had just fallen and Communist dictatorships were toppling like diseased trees exposed to the fresh winds of approaching democracy.

All of this was happening a long way from Saudi Arabia, but the events still had dramatic consequences for the country and other dictatorships that had profited from the partition of the world during the Cold War.

Up until the time when the Berlin Wall was dismantled, even the western part of a divided Germany had learnt to live in a divided country in a divided Europe. It was not the rigid politics of the Western governments, but the weak economies of the Eastern European countries and the determination of the people, that succeeded in transforming the European world that had existed for decades.

Even though they do not like to be reminded of it, it was a fact that Western governments had treated democracies and dictatorships equally. There is only one reason for this – the quest for stability; the hope that such an attitude would prevent war. For decades, democratically elected governments accepted the claims of legitimacy and equality put forward by both the political and military dictatorships of the world. It was only when the oppressed nations of the other side of the Iron Curtain began to rebel against dictatorship that the West allowed itself to be reminded of the criminal nature of these regimes. It was the people who brought down the wall. The Polish showed the way with their demands for a free and independent union, Solidarity, which in turn produced the first free president, Lech Walesa. In Czechoslovakia other 'dissidents' paved the way for the creation of a new democracy and a new president, Vaclac Havel. In East and Central Europe, movements led by other proud representatives of freedom helped to bring about democracy and move dictatorships out of the region. The deciding factor was the impoverished economies of the countries and their inability to stand up to Western competition. The desire for freedom demonstrated its strength the day Boris Yeltsin climbed one of the military tanks driving through the streets of Moscow and managed to stop a desperate attempt by totalitarian forces to retrieve their power.

This was not a victory for Western ideology, even though some self-assured entities in the West who liked to believe this was the case. The ultimate victor was the idea of the right to freedom and access to human rights for everyone.

The truth is that four decades before, the governments of the East, West, South and the North had endorsed the Universal Declaration of Human Rights. The beginning of the 1990s saw the declaration put to the test, even though the rulers of Saudi Arabia would much prefer to have been left out of any experiments in democracy. The ruling Saud family had secured a firm alliance with the West, but just like the old Eastern dictatorships they had also insisted on equal status for local traditions and the ruling system. Local spokesmen for union organisations similar to the ones that brought Lech Walesa to power were locked up. Local dissidents of Havel's stature were subjected to torture and thrown into prison long before they could publish their books.

Since then, there have been anti-totalitarian movements worldwide. Ordinary citizens demand to be heard, to share the power, to secure the right to freedom. This is not only happening in a small group of Eastern European countries, but all over the world. In 1989, the same spirit of rebellion led young people in China to demand the right to freedom on Tianenmen Square in Beijing. This encouraged the Burmese to revolt in Rangoon and Serb students to do the same in Belgrade.

A number of these demands have been heard in Saudi Arabia. The priests have resisted the authorities' attempt to censor the mosques and used their Friday sermons to protest against government policies. Complaints are made of corruption and hypocrisy and young liberals are demanding the right to influence governmental administration. Business people are demanding a more liberal attitude to foreign trade. All these demands are, however, met with censorship, arbitrary arrests and brutal reprisals.

There are no rights in Saudi Arabia. No one has the right to criticise the government, to demand a free press, to put forward claims in the mosques, to organise unions, to demonstrate; it is all strictly forbidden by the law laid down by the Saud family.

Is it really possible for a country or a dynasty to withdraw from the rest of the world? Can the rulers of one nation deliberately choose to be international social outcasts? Theoretically, the Saud family are bound by the principles of the United Nations' Universal Declaration on Human Rights, although there was opposition from the family when the other governments of the United Nations passed the resolution. Nevertheless, Saudi Arabia is indirectly under an obligation to abide by the principles of the declaration partly because the country is a member of the United Nations, partly because it endorsed the International Declaration at the human rights conference in Vienna in 1993.

In reality, the rulers of Saudi Arabia have voluntarily chosen the role of social outcast, outside international law. Out of the 25 important international 'instruments' in the field of human rights, Saudi Arabia has only signed three: the prohibition of genocide and slavery and the exploitation of children. As far as the rest of the 'instruments' other states have endorsed in the United Nations' register, Saudi Arabia's consent is conspicuously absent. The Riyadh dynasty has neither signed the treaty of civil and political rights nor that pertaining to economic, social and cultural rights; furthermore the Saud family have not conceded to the convention on the abolition of all forms of racial discrimination. Neither has it signed the convention of the abolition of discrimination against women, the prohibition against torture or that of the rights of refugees.

On the contrary, the government in Riyadh chooses to use repressive measures and censorship as political weapons. Other governments have also tried to do this, for instance the Soviet Union and the countries of the Eastern Block before the fall of the Berlin Wall. Other kinds of repression was practised in South Africa.

The Universal Declaration of Human Rights is based on the idea of worldwide human equality. The outbreak of anti-totalitarian movements at the end of the Cold War gave impetus to the fulfillment of this idea in practice. But the kingdom of Saudi Arabia has no other constitution than its own interpretation of Sharia, the law of Islam. The realities of daily life could be paraphrased in a law as follows:

> Saudi Arabia – absolute monarchy. The King has absolute power and can select his own crown prince from within the family ranks. No free elections and as far as legal rights are concerned women are second-class citizens. Freedom of speech does not exist and political and union activity are forbidden. There is no religious liberty and torture is standard punishment . . .

Each and every one of these points is inconsistent with international law and negates the dream of a common code of human rights. Nevertheless, in the United Nations system only governments apply for the membership card, not people. This puts the world in somewhat of a dilemma: whether to show consideration for the ruling dictatorships or for the oppressed citizen. This is where the United Nations Commission in Geneva comes in.

Every year at the end of winter, the Commission meets at the Palais des Nations to make a careful assessment of the state of the world with regards to human rights. Here, citizens from all parts of the world gather to lodge complaints about their respective governments. In principle the system is the same as that used in democratic national law where citizens with a grievance has the right to initiate legal proceedings, judged by a court of law; the same procedure is used in Geneva on an international level. In Europe, the European Human Rights Commission? in Strasbourg is used to bring governments before the court if their citizens claim they have been unjustly treated by the national court of law. All citizens have the right to this court of appeal by virtue of their countries affiliation with the European Convention of Human Rights. Today, after the fall of the Berlin Wall, the leaders of 39 states are prepared to meet their citizens' demands for political accountability. Turkey, a Muslim country, has granted its citizens individual access to this international court of law.

Every year citizens of Saudi Arabia come to the UN Commission in Geneva to lodge complaints against the authorities in Riyadh. Their largest obstacle is that the Saud family have neither endorsed the convention nor the complaints procedure. The following statement from a diplomat, who has followed the negotiations in Geneva for years is an accurate description of the situation: 'This means that the United Nations can only work with Saudi Arabia's indirect acceptance of the Universal Declaration of Human Rights and the United Nations' general references to 'human rights'.

Before the Gulf War and the end of the Cold War it was easy for the Saud dynasty to escape criticism. The Soviet Union protected its allies in the Third World as did the USA. The latter's allies included Saudi Arabia. Regional blocks, for example the Arab countries, protected one another from close scrutiny and this is probably the reason why no verdict reached before the Gulf War ever subjected Iraq to criticism for its gross violation of human rights. Since the war, Iraq has been subject to close and uncompromising investigations which have revealed political crimes that could have been exposed even before Saddam Hussein sent his troops into Kuwait.

Even in the 1990s the international community has resorted to superficial strategies in the name of expediency. Every year several states, including Iran and Iraq, are openly criticised and some have been the subject of 'special observation', for example Cuba, Afghanistan, Burma, ex-Yugoslavia, Zaire, Rwanda, Burundi and several others. In contrast, up until 1997, Saudi Arabia escaped criticism due to the protection by the USA. However, as a European diplomat in Geneva states, 'Saudi Arabia cannot continue to get away with it.' The country, that is to say the Saud family, has for several years been pulled into what is known as 'the 1503 procedure'. This consists of a series of discussions behind closed doors between representatives of the 53 members of the United Nations Commission. These discussions have gradually revealed a systematic pattern of gross violations of human rights. As the same diplomat states, 'It is very difficult to avoid the issue of Saudi Arabia due to the constant accusations of torture and other violations of human rights. In 1996 it was decided to maintain close observation of four countries in particular – Saudi Arabia, Chad, Sierra Leone and Uzbekistan.'

At the same time a group of European countries issued a warning that they were prepared to back the appointment of a 'special observer' to report on developments in Saudi Arabia and the instigation of a procedure that would force that country into the open where it would be possible to pass (usually critical) resolutions. In a letter to the Commission, the Saudi Arabian ambassador at the United Nations in Geneva announced that his country was under no obligation to co-operate with the Commission since it had not signed the UN's treaties. Despite this, as the representative of a global conscience, the Commission still feels under an obligation to work for the benefit of the citizens of Saudi Arabia. Unlike the Saud family, the commission in Geneva has to try to fulfil its obligations.

Whether or not the Saud family has signed the UN treaties, the fundamental problem remains: is it acceptable that the citizens of some countries have fewer rights to legal protection or equality than those of other countries? If a European state wrote in its constitution or penal code that Muslims did not have the right to organise, it would not only be regarded as discrimination (since Christians and Jews and all others have the right to form unions or associations) but also as a violation of Muslim human rights. Is the discrimination or the violation any less because it happens in Saudi Arabia?

For the Saud family the problem is exacerbated by the fact that more than 20 Muslim governments have introduced a law based on the International Covenant of Civil and Political Rights – and regard it as fully consistent with the fundamental precepts of their religion. As early as the 1970s the Saud family made an attempt to combat this growing tendency by sponsoring work on what was to be the 'Cairo Declaration of Human Rights in Islam'. In this, human rights are considered of secondary importance compared to the law of Islam, the Sharia.

But deference to cultural differences can never justify the erosion of unquestionable universal laws such as the prohibition of torture. 'Different nations can clearly adopt different attitudes to the meting out of punishment but not to the question of guilt. And the whole foundation of these universal laws is that no citizen of any country should be subjected to torture or other violations of human rights, irrespective of gender, colour or religion', says a legal advisor on human rights in Geneva.

This is the legal position. The international 'instruments' for the protection of human rights have been approved by world governments and no state is seriously going to suggest that the work should be undone. Added to this is the moral issue. It may be that governments find it difficult to adhere to some of the rules and feel subjected to moral pressure. But this is exactly the object of the exercise.

CHAPTER SEVEN

Protector of the Holy Cities

Afraid of Islamists

'I never heard anyone regret a single day they had spent on Jihad, nor anyone contemplate whether the Jihad had been the cause of the pain they were subjected to by those who do not fear Allah.'

Who is speaking? It is an anonymous voice on the Internet on 11 November 1996 – one of the voices the Saudis would definitely prefer not to have appearing on the computer monitors of their citizens: 'An Arab Afghan'. This is how the man presents himself, most likely one of the thousands of brave, proud Arabs who launched themselves into a bloody, tenacious 'holy war' or Jihad in order to liberate Afghanistan from the Soviet army of occupation. They stole into Afghanistan via Pakistan without much more preparation than good will, their strong faith and exceptional solidarity. They fought in brutal cold and baking heat, often only with hand weapons and grenades, against the heavily equipped Soviet army. Despite all material disadvantages, they contributed to procuring the freedom of Afghanistan in 1992, at least from foreign occupation, and they did Islam credit. Why, then, should they 'regret' or 'contemplate' their efforts?

His past in Afghanistan seems to have been the reason why, in late November 1995, 11 agents of 'Mabaheth', Saudi intelligence, bulldozed their way through his door in Jedda in western Saudi Arabia. He was not the only one to get a visit. All over the country, 'Arab Afghans' were sought out and arrested in unknown numbers after a powerful bomb in Riyadh had killed five US soldiers. The 'Arab Afghan' on the Internet had only just managed to get up on his crutches – he was minus one leg – before they smashed in the door and carried him off to the ar-Ruwais prison at the headquarters of the security services.

Neither the Internet nor 'Mabaheth' can be consulted for verification, and the US police were not allowed access either to the many people arrested after the bombing or to the four men who were later convicted and beheaded. But what the Afghan Arab has to tell is like an echo of the other reports that slip out of Saudi prisons. Like other sources who have experienced the prisons and whom I have spoken to personally, he says he was locked into a cell that was no bigger than one metre by a metre and a half (others have called it the 'dog kennel'). He spent three months there under regular torture. He says,

'I denied having had any links whatsoever with the bombing. That was the truth. I didn't know any more about the bomb than I'd seen and heard in the media.

They beat me wildly, not one part of my body was spared. All my clothes were torn to shreds. During all this my hands were still cuffed. Their appetite for torture increased as they saw the state I was in. They started to use whips and implements I had never seen in my life before.

After thrashing me for several hours they asked again and again, "Why did you bomb Riyadh?"

I could do nothing but deny the charge . . . The next day they came to get me for further interrogation. They asked the same questions all over again. Every time I refused to admit to it they hit me with a whip. And then they tried a new form of torture. My arms were bound behind my back and was hung up by a metal bar like a slaughtered animal ready for roasting.'

In the prison he would meet other Arab Mujaheddin, holy warriors from the years in Afghanistan. Their courage when faced by the torturers fills him with pride. On the other hand, he was enraged by the way his tormentors desecrated the scholarly Muslim clerics and Sharia, Islamic law itself. These are serious accusations against 'the king's torturers and servants' – the former prisoner, now Internet writer makes, is calling Saudi Arabia a 'prison for those who want reform or pay homage to Islamic law'.

King Fahad, the King and official 'Protector of the two holy cities of Mecca and Medina', in March 1992, said 'Now as ever, the kingdom is committed to God's laws.' Fahad made a long speech to his people, whom he promised the establishment of a consultative assembly. 'Citizens,' he said, 'with God's help, we will continue in line with Islam, in co-operation with those who want only good for Islam and all Muslims . . . intent on securing progress for this country and happiness for its people.'

Every Friday, people throughout Saudi Arabia go to prayer. All the nation's 11,000 mosques assemble the population in the heartland of Islam. It is the most important day of the week, but a trying one for the security services. Every single cleric has to have his speech approved. But the security service people take no chances, they are listening everywhere. The clergy may be state employees, and Saudi Arabia may officially be an Islamic state, but the family does not feel entirely happy about the mosques, the only places where people are permitted to gather in large numbers. They are not allowed to strike or demonstrate, to organize themselves and certainly not meet in large groups, neither at work nor in the streets. But Friday prayers is when they all get together, the linch of the Islamic state and the soft target for the security services.

The very fact that the mosques are allowed to assemble citizens and to give them time to exchange views, in addition to praying, affords them an even greater role in the kingdom. This is where the rumour of the week is passed on, where popular temperaments can run free and – to the terror of the security services – this is where criticism can be formulated and fed back to the bazaar. Orthodox priests were the first, and certainly the most eager, to criticize in their mosques the arrival of non-Muslim soldiers in the kingdom during the Gulf War. The security services immediately stepped in a put and stop to this, only to find that the forbidden sermons turned up on illegal tapes throughout the land, recorded clandestinely by Muslim preachers whom the 'Islamic state' does not allow to speak freely.

Millions of the world's Muslims meet every year at the traditional pilgrimage, the Hajjs to the common meeting place of Muslim society, *ummah.* Just like Friday prayers, the Hajj ought to be among Saudi Arabia's finest days. All the same, this very pilgrimage has given the Saud family many a grey hair and caused much concern. It represents everything that Saudi Arabia does not applaud. Massive crowds of people in one place, crowds moving in and out of the country – what could be worse? Time for dialogue and the absorption of ideas; and worse still, these Muslims come from different backgrounds, each with their own interpretation of Islam and the traditions of the Prophet.

'If the pilgrimage to the Arafat Plain outside Mecca is not to serve as an opportunity to gather in common concern for Muslims in need, what then is left of the true significance of the pilgrimage?', asked *Crescent International*, a news magazine published by an Islamic movement in Pakistan and Canada. Like Iran and radical Muslim movements, 'Crescent' demands that Saudi Arabia should be relieved of its control of the pilgrimage and – exactly as had been contemplated in the 1920s – Mecca be made an international Islamic zone. The annual get-together should serve to mobilise Muslims against international injustice.

Saudi Arabia's ruling family will have none of that, neither internationalization nor the use of the Hajj for political ends, especially not after Iranian pilgrims in 1987 used the Hajj to demonstrate – and later to clash with Saudi soldiers in a blood bath that cost 400 people their lives.

It is outrageous, that Saudi Arabia should still be allowed to dominate the pilgrimage and decide how many pilgrims individual countries can send to Mecca, wrote *Crescent* in the winter of 1996–97. The magazine reminded readers in an editorial that Muslims in Chechenia, Bosnia, Kashmir, Palestine and on the Philippine island of Mindanao and other points of focus had been killed without Muslims gathered in Mecca having a chance to discuss it. 'Allah's enemies can kill as they deem fit, but Muslims cannot defend themselves. They are not even permitted to talk about such things in the house of Allah! But did Allah not command that his faithful should fight if they came under attack?', asks the magazine, which is banned in Saudi Arabia.

Two hundred years have passed since the Saud family allied themselves with the preacher Muhammed bin Abdul-Wahab and his dogmatic interpretation of the holy book. And the alliance between the dynasty and the scribes – *ulema* – is applauded in Saudi scriptures as the kingdom's assurance of a just, god-fearing society.

From this to the king taking on responsibility for the clergy and religious judges is a far cry. Neither the dynasty nor the king have imagined they would go that far. The king appoints the senior *ulema* and has the right to dismiss and replace them. His government appoint and pay the ordinary clergy. His intelligence services keep their eyes on them. No ordinary court, manned by ordinary scholars of the Koran and Islamic law, has the right to bring royalty before it. For this to occur, special courts are required, which have the King as their absolute superior.

Is it an 'Islamic society' that permits a totally uneducated secular monarch to pronounce himself supreme religious leader, the chief of scholars who have studied far longer than he has, and of the entire priesthood and the Bench, the military and the government? The dynasty has never asked the people of Saudi Arabia. But the regime's latent fear of what goes on in the mosques is proof of Saudi apprehension regarding the legitimacy of the royal family. Can it be right that the Islamic state fear Islamists? Perhaps the state isn't 'Islamic' after all, but simply an absolute monarchy clinging to Islam when it suits the dynasty, setting itself above religion when its suits it even better.

It is religious activists in particular who end up in Saudi prisons as political prisoners. According to practically every international human rights organization they are tortured in large numbers to force them to make a confession whether they committed a crime or not. They are not allowed access to a defence lawyer and have no means of complaining about the torture to which they are subjected.

As the 'Arab Afghan' quoted earlier says,

'I realised after being transferred to a collective cell that the number of prisoners of conscience there was extremely large. It was as though any young man who showed an inkling of religious devotion was incarcerated in ar-Ruwais prison. I discovered that the wives of some of them were also behind bars. They were interrogated by *wuhush ad-dhariah* [wild monsters] . . . some prisoners told me how they had been threatened with the rape of their *mahrems* [wives, mothers or sisters] if they did not confess. I also discovered that many prisoners were herded into one room, all naked, where they were tortured while the others looked on so as further to humiliate and degrade them.'

He continues:

'When my interrogators realised that I had no links with the bombing in Riyadh, they started trying to get me to confess to being among the people in "Takfir", those that not only say that our leaders are infidels but even go as far as to claim that the *ulema* and society as a whole are godless (which would make it legitimate to start a war against them according to the Sharia). They wanted me to confess to having used weapons against some civilian areas.'

The political prisoners have very rarely used violent means. Most of them have used a means much more dangerous to the royal family – words. The 'Islamic state' has therefore deemed it necessary to lock up clergy because it could not tolerate their sermons. It has incarcerated religious activists, who during Friday prayers or at the bazaar have disseminated the view that the royal family does not abide by the dictates of Islam and is not worthy of power.

The new Islamists are the Saudis' greatest threat. If only a few more of them used violence, the ruling dynasty would have a more legitimate reason to campaign for their arrest. But the opposition is to a predominant degree, non-violent. What is worse, it is religious and has a solid basis from which to contest the validity of the royal family's power. This is far more dangerous, for these are people who know the Koran by heart, who refuse to accept the royals' corrupted lifestyle.

◆◆◆

Although two hundred years have passed since the Saud family adopted Wahhabism in its struggle for power in the Arab Peninsular, it has not been in a position either to follow the sect's puritan rules or to unify the entire Muslim community in present-day Saudi Arabia. Some 6 to 8 per cent of the population are not Sunni Muslims, like the majority, but Shias. In the eastern province where the largest oil reserves are hidden beneath the sand and sea, the Shia even constitute a vulnerable half of the population. They are misunderstood for their different attitude to Islam and partly feared as potential friends of Shia-Muslim Iran. For some of their activists this has led to death. 'On 3 September 1992,' writes Amnesty International of one such victim. Abdul-Karim Malallah was publicly beheaded, in al-Qatif having been found guilty of atheism and blasphemy.' Sadiq Malallah, a Shia Muslim, was arrested in April 1988 and was first accused of having thrown a stone at a police patrol. According to reports he was held in isolation for long periods during the first months of his captivity and tortured prior to his first appearance before a judge in July 1988. The judge accused him of smuggling bibles into Saudi Arabia, which he denied. He was then asked to convert to Wahhabism, but he declined. He was kept at the Mabahith al-Amma prison in al-Damman until April 1990, when he was transferred to the Mabahith al-Amma in Riyadh where he remained until his execution. Sadiq Malallah is believed to have been involved in an attempt to secure improved rights for Saudi Arabia's Shia Muslim minority.

The death sentence that cost Sadiq Malallah his head – presumably on a public square after Friday prayers – can be traced back to Sheikh Abdul-Aziz bin Abdullah bin Baz, Saudi Arabia's supreme religious leader, whose powers are only exceeded by those of the king. Sheikh Baz has declared that Shia Muslims are atheists. In his fatwa, or religious ruling, number 2008, he deems it illegal for Sunni Muslims to marry Shias. Another member of the king's 'Council of Senior Ulema' has called the Shia Muslims' way of slaughtering animals and their meat as impure and illegal.

Shia Muslims are also discriminated against in their application for jobs at state offices and companies. While it is forbidden to attempt to convert a Sunni Muslim to another faith, and punishable by death for a Muslim to forsake Islam, the Saud regime actively encourages the conversion of Shia Muslims. Books by the Shia Muslim leader Sheikh Hasan Musa al-Safar have been banned. This includes his work *al-Huriyya wal-Ta'adudiyya fil Islam* (*Freedom and Pluralism in Islam*).

One of the occurrences that plague the conscience of the royal family must surely be the occupation in 1979 of the Grand Mosque in Mecca. It had to be liberated – with the help of Christian French soldiers – during a massive military operation following which the king was sent the 63 surviving occupants to lose their heads on public squares and streets.

The challenge faced by the royal family today is much more threatening. The new political Islamists are clergy, highly educated university people and young students who contest the validity of the dynasty's right to administer the kingdom's income. They demand greater openness, greater responsibility on the part of the government and less dependence on the world outside if they are to be taken seriously as 'Protectors of the Two Holy Cities of Mecca and Medina'. To a certain extent, an entirely new class has emerged which is demanding influence, in reality auguring a challenge that will come from a growing middle class and a new intellectual elite not prepared simply to follow 'as the King deems fit'.

When Islamists in May 1991 wrote an unusual 'open letter' to the King, they demanded an 'independent' consultative assembly with the power to do more than simply counsel; they demanded the repeal of laws not in harmony with Sharia (in itself a hefty criticism of the kingdom); with a veiled, though recognizable, criticism of corruption within the power apparatus; they demanded that all citizens be equal before the law; greater social equality and last but by no means least, independence for the courts. A band of liberal academics had already written their own open letter demanding respect for human rights, including rights for women.

The liberal letter was more or less ignored, while the 'religious' letter created quite a stir, also among the state funded clerics. Sheikh bin Baz publicly denounced the religious letter as an 'insult to His Majesty the King. Baz was in the firing line himself at one stage because he, to the chagrin of the new Islamists, had given his blessing to the King's invitation of foreign military forces to Saudi Arabian soil. And a year later he received, in September, a new letter from the intrepid Islamists who had demanded that the law be brought into line with the official dogma of Saudi Arabia as an Islamic state. They demanded freedom for all Muslim clerics to publish books, to preach and to write; the potential for priests to participate in the work of government, a ban on Western secular laws; restriction of the rights of the police, lawyers for the accused; for torture to be outlawed; supervision of the government's budget and accounts via the consultative assembly, and so on.

Bin Baz, not surprisingly, was furious and wanted the Council of Senior Clerics to denounce these independent Islamists. Seven of the Council's 17 members would, however, not sign the denunciation, an act which humiliated their leader. As a demonstration of where power really resides, King Fahad dismissed the seven and had them replaced with authoritarian priests. A year later, Fahad appointed the members of his New Consultative Council, Majlis al-Shoura, leaving no doubt, however, that the Council's role was only consultative. This dynasty does not relax its grip on power at a stroke – not even to Islamists in the Islamic state.

Women

Just half of the population

The Saudi Arabian diplomat asked his wife to drive me home; that made her laugh. An extremely intelligent woman, a skilful driver, her long brown hair gathered into an old-fashioned bun at the nape of her neck. If at home in Riyadh she would, for this action, be arrested, beaten with bamboo rods and probably thrown into prison. She would be accused of a long list of criminal offences and the most serious would be that she had been caught on her own with a man who was neither her husband nor a male relative. Nor had she covered up her beautiful hair or her legs; her tartan kilt only reached to just below the knee. To cap it all she was sitting behind a steering wheel.

Saudi Arabian law states that a woman must cover herself ensuring that her neck, hair, arms and legs do not reveal any of her beauty so as to arouse the desire of the opposite sex. Women are not allowed in the streets on their own; they must be accompanied by a brother, a husband or other women. A woman is not allowed to drive a car and can only travel by car if driven by a male relative or a chauffeur. Is it really Islam that forbids women to drive cars? If so, Muslim countries all over the world must be breaking Islamic law. Women drive cars in Iran, in Bangladesh, in Malaysia and in the rest of the Arab world.

Although it attracts a great deal of attention internationally, whether or not they are allowed to drive a car is probably not the most important issue for Saudi Arabian women, but it is important indeed. On the evening of 6 November 1990, 46 women took part in a drive-yourself demonstration that succeeded in highlighting the legal rights position of Saudi Arabian women. The women had previously arranged with their chauffeurs to drive them over to the Tamimi supermarket in Riyadh. This happened right in the middle of 'Operation Desert Shield', the international build-up of troops in Saudi Arabia called in to ensure that Saddam Hussein's Iraqi troops, having occupied Kuwait in August, did not move further south to the oil fields of Saudi Arabia. Among the several hundred thousand foreign soldiers moving onto Saudi Arabian soil were thousands of US women soldiers. However, unlike her and her 46 sisters in Riyadh on 6 November, the tough US women soldiers were allowed to drive cars through the streets of Saudi Arabia.

For Saudi Arabian society this was a radical change in policy and for the most conservative of the priests it only confirmed suspicions that the Saud family had allied themselves with godless Westerners. For the more liberal of the female population, such a move also confirmed the fact that law and tradition is a question of interpretation. All in all, this was precisely what the Saud family had done. It was evidence of the fact that when the ruling powers felt threatened, they were willing to stretch a point, even if it meant that the protectors of the two holy cities should put themselves under the protection of tough truck-driving women in trousers, with rings in their ears and crucifixes round their necks, inside their shirts.

For the women at the supermarket the point of the demonstration was not to ally themselves with the American women soldiers driving camouflaged trucks. These Saudi Arabian women, all veiled according to regulations, had enough to deal with just by driving their own Mercedes Benzs, Lincolns, Buicks and other models through the streets of Riyadh. They had previously sent a flood of telegrams to the authorities and the press in which they made it quite clear that they were demonstrating as true patriots in the interests of Saudi Arabia alone.

'It is vital that the authorities understand that as educated women we have driven our own vehicles during the course of our university studies abroad and that we cannot accept being dependent on someone to drive us around,' said one of the demonstrators to a reporter from the *New York Times*. 'Apart from being a humiliating experience it is also against the law, since Islam says that a woman must not be left alone with a man who is not a relative of hers. But this is precisely what happens when I am driven around in my car by a man from Pakistan or the Sudan or any other chauffeur. It is also very expensive for the family budget.'

The women therefore asked their drivers to step out of the car and one after the other they positioned themselves behind the steering wheel; in many of the cars the other seats were occupied by daughters, sisters and women friends. All of them were used to sitting behind a steering wheel, most of them had their driving licences with them, albeit licences issued abroad, mainly in the USA and Europe. This cortege which moved slowly through the streets of Riyadh that evening, would not have attracted much attention in other Muslim countries, neither in the Arab world or in the Muslim world at large. But in Saudi Arabia the powers believe that they know better, despite the fact that they were willing to yield a point and bend the rules in a time of crisis.

In any case the drive was a short one. It came to an abrupt and certainly symbolic end in King Abdel Aziz Road, where the Muttawa – the King's religious police force – while screaming 'whores' at the women inside the cars, forced the procession to a halt by banging and hammering on the doors and windows. The demonstration was over.

'A lot of the women were from well-respected families with excellent connections, some even to the royal family itself', says a sister of one of the demonstrators, from a city somewhere in the Arab world. However, connections or not, the authorities thought it neither funny nor convincing, even if the women had made a point of calling the demonstration 'patriotic'. As early as a week afterwards, the Ministry of the Interior – the central 'ministry for law and order' – issued a formal ban on women driving. This was now written into the law, whereas previously it had only been banned according to custom. The ministry did not waste much time. It was now proclaimed that 'Women are strictly forbidden to drive cars in this kingdom and whosoever disregards this ban will be severely punished.' Apparently the ban was the result of a fatwa, a religious ruling, issued by Saudi Arabia's highest ecclesiastical figure, Sheikh Abdul Aziz bin Abdullah bin Baz. Of course the ban did not apply to the female American soldiers.

In contrast, the demonstration ended badly for the Saudi Arabian women. They were all dragged off to the police station where their husbands or male relatives were forced to sign statements promising that the women would never take part in a demonstration again or even talk about the event. Most of the women were then forced to relinquish their passports and all those who were public employees were sacked. Among these were several University lecturers such as Dr Suad al Mane, Fawzia el-Bakr, Dr Mowadda and Dr Suad al-Mane. The story appeared in the international press but Saudi Arabian newspapers did not cover it. It was a year before the women were given back their passports. Many of their partners were prevented from travelling out of the country for several years.

Apart from the ban on the company of male strangers and on car driving, women are also segregated on public transport and are expected to use special doors, usually those at the back of the bus. If they are public employees they are also relegated to specific offices.

No woman can leave Saudi Arabia without her husband's consent. As it says in the *Human Rights Yearbook* issued by the State Department 'women have very few political and social rights and are not treated as equal members of society'. In Saudi Arabia it is difficult to do anything about this denial of rights. Women's movements or organisations are against the law. Women are neither represented in the government nor on the Advisory Council and it is forbidden to criticise this legal discrimination.

As soon as they leave their homes they are forced by law to wear their black *abaya*, a large piece of black cloth used to cover the body, another to cover the head, hair, neck and the bottom half of the face. For a woman in Saudi Arabia this is not just traditional dress, it is also a very practical piece of clothing which can be used to conceal both her clothes and purchases or forbidden goods such as illegal magazines, tape recordings of excommunicated priests and dubious video films that the Muttawa should not see.

In the courts the legal system is based on classical Islamic justice, the Sharia, and no contemporary interpretations are allowed. It takes two women's testimonies to offset a man's. For a woman, hospital treatment is also impossible unless she is accompanied to the hospital by a male relative.

Saudi Arabian men are allowed to marry up to four women as long as they can support them and can divorce every one of them by merely repeating the phrase 'I divorce you' three times. In contrast a Saudi Arabian woman can only divorce once and it is a long and complicated judicial procedure. A man has the right as well to enter into several 'short-term marriages', in which he can receive sexual favours from a woman he does not know, despite the fact that official prostitution is banned and a criminal offence; as so often happens there is a difference between what the law says and what happens in practice. Instead of a red light area where the prostitutes are easily recognisable, Muslim 'ladies of the night' are found in more anonymous districts or supermarkets. According to sources from within the ranks of the royal princes, it is not unheard of for those in power to make use of such services. Drunkenness and lechery is not limited to the country's subjects, unlike punishment for these offences.

◆◆◆

The key word is separation. Both on the street and in public buildings, in education and in private business, the authorities insist on maintaining a total division between men and women. Cafes and restaurants must be equipped with special 'family rooms' if women are to be allowed in, and mosques keep separate sections for men and women to pray. The same policy of separation is practised in banks, ministries and shops. Nowhere can women decide for themselves; everything is controlled by the monarchy.

Women are allowed to own property, shops and businesses and they also have the right to buy shares in them. However, even though a woman may own the bulk of the shares, she is obliged to ask a man to represent her at board meetings or the like. If she owns a shop that has both male and female customers she cannot work in the shop and is obliged to employ a male shop assistant.

From early childhood, girls are educated separately in single sex schools. This continues until the time they can apply for a place in one of Saudi Arabia's seven universities who accept female students. There they are educated separately, in some cases by men who give lectures using video transmission from another room.

The population are constantly being reminded that this is how it should be in a true Islamic society. Nevertheless, the more conservative sultanate of neighbouring Oman has several women police officers patrolling the street of Muscat and at least two women serving on Sultan Qaboos' Advisory Council, the Majlis al-Shoura. The press of the Kuwait emirate prints lively political discussions and opinions from both men and women, as to whether the latter should be allowed the vote and given access to the Danish designed parliament by the sea front. All around the Gulf and on the other side, in Iran, women drive cars. Does this make them less Islamic?

Saudi Arabia stubbornly refuses to accept any other version of Islam than their own, which is the one the preacher Mohammed Ibn Abdel Wahab agreed on with the Saud lineage in the 1700s. This interpretation adopts a position reconcilable with the country's ruling principle – that the state is responsible for the maintenance of religious Puritanism. In practice it does nothing more than prevent the women of the kingdom from discussing the systems of other Muslim countries and the position of women within them. Interpretation is a man's prerogative.

Until the 1960s women had no access to any forms of education other than training in the Koran at private Koran schools. It was during the reign of King Faisal that one of his wives persuaded her husband to open a school for girls, Dar al-Hanan in Jedda; with the aim of training more efficient housewives. The idea of educating girls was not received with equal enthusiasm in all parts of the country. In a few towns such as the highly conservative Burayda, the proposal was met with violent protests. Despite the fact that there is a significant difference between quality of staff and teaching in the girls' and boys' schools – and in the universities – most girls in Saudi Arabia now receive at least a basic education. Moreover, the rate of illiteracy has been drastically reduced in line with Saudi Arabia's impressive social and economic development. In following this new policy the government is sowing the seeds of its own downfall. More and more young people are demanding better education without being given access to qualified jobs or the right to greater participation and influence in the running of their country. Women are not allowed to study subjects that are important politically and economically for Saudi Arabia, such as geology, engineering and law. Neither are they allowed to study abroad unless accompanied by a male relative.

◆◆◆

In a world that is becoming more and more international, Saudi Arabia still avoids contact with the outside world. Secure in the interpretation of its own values it is nevertheless concerned about their viability in a modern world.

More than 75,000 young Saudi Arabians are thought to have completed a university education in the USA where they have been exposed to other interpretations of the law and other cultures. They return home with new ideas and attitudes that are not necessarily compatible with the Saud family's vision of the future.

On the face of it the media of Saudi Arabia is derogatory about Western cultural influence and any meeting with Westerners or the Western media has been strictly controlled and censored for years. However, if we take into account the progress being made in other Muslim societies and the widening debate on political influence and equality for women, the Muslim world in itself represents an increasingly pressing challenge for the supremacy of the Saud family.

Far from all the young active women of Saudi Arabia turn their backs on tradition and orthodoxy. As is happening among the predominantly male opposition, Saudi Arabia is now experiencing a religious revival within the ranks of the female critics of the monarchy. They dismiss the disapproval of the outside world and are scornfully critical of demonstrations in the form of motor cavalcades, which they view as blind acceptance of Western values. They do, however, criticise the monarchy for immoral leadership and they wear their *abayas* with pride as a symbol of a new form of social identity. They would not approve of the Saudi Arabian diplomat's wife who throws her *abaya* and all her other customs away as soon as she steps out of the Saudi plane somewhere in Europe.

CHAPTER NINE

Torture

No redress

'Remember, we need the Saudis more than they need us.' Keith Carmichael will never forget that remark, perhaps the last thing he expected to hear when in late January 1982 – after 84 days of humiliating imprisonment and sadistic torture – he received a visit in prison from the British vice-consul in Riyadh. He relates the episode quite calmly, although still somewhat perturbed after all those years. Carmichael had been expecting an expression of concern, also of anger, on the part of his country's official representative.

But just like the Egyptian doctor, Dr Mohammed al-Khalifa, Keith Carmichael had a lot to learn both about Saudi Arabia and his own country's fearful respect for the Big Brother of the Arab world. Twenty or so years previously, a British defence attaché in Jordan had asked Carmichael to spy on the Saudi military installations in the north-western part of the kingdom, a request he had politely ignored. Now in early 1982, he had to fear rotting away in a Saudi prison, called the 'civil rights centre' while British officials turned their backs on him.

No fate could come as more of a surprise for Keith

Carmichael, then a 47 year-old, handsome Scottish businessman, a son of the British upper middle class. He was educated at England's best schools, received a military training at Sandhurst and had served in the British Scots Guards in Jordan as a National Service Officer. Lawrence of Arabia had been his childhood hero, and Oxford University the home of his youth. But now, when he most needed his friends in London's upper class clubs, he had to take a lesson in *realpolitik* instead.

Keith Carmichael was aware that life in Saudi Arabia could be dangerous. He had heard about public executions after Friday prayers and the lopping off of hands and feet, and read about them in the newspapers. He had seen the Muttawa, the brutal so-called religious police in the streets. But he had also experienced the discreet charm of upper-class living, which allows the brotherhood of the power elite to drink themselves senseless while the Muttawa on the street outside was arresting ordinary people for the very same transgression.

Carmichael had enjoyed alcohol with one of the king's brothers. He had never been first to raise the glass, always allowing the Saudi to be the first. He had witnessed many princes drinking alcohol. He had been drinking with royal friends outside Saudi Arabia, seen one of the king's blood brothers drink himself out of his senses on an Air France flight out of the country and seen prostitutes coming and going from the prince's suite somewhere in Europe.

But Keith Carmichael was not one of them. In mid-October 1981 he fled in his Nissan 4x4. He drove out of Riyadh towards the east, into the desert which separates the kingdom of Saudi Arabia from Qatar. He feared for his life.

Not that Carmichael had committed any crime from which he had to flee, unless of course one included his experience of the royal family's own excesses. Carmichael was fleeing from one man in particular, Prince Saud Abdullah al Faisal, grandson of former King Faisal and a man with extremely close links with everything linked to the power in Saudi Arabia. His great-uncle Fahad, who a few years later would accede to the throne, was then crown prince. Another distant uncle was defence minister, yet another interior minister, and one was governor of the capital, Riyadh.

Prince Saud, whom Keith Carmichael had got to know at Sandhurst, had been a useful contact for Sacem International NV, where Carmichael drew his salary as director in Riyadh. Sacem carried out both contracting and consultancy work in Saudi Arabia, all with the Saudi company Sigma as legal sponsor in the country. The head of Sigma was Prince Saud, who for a 5 per cent commission made sure that Sacem secured contacts and made sure that all the necessary paperwork and licences were in order. This type of commission butters the bread of Saudi Arabian princes.

In early October, however, Prince Saud's appetite for commission exceeded his ability to acquire Saudi buyers of Sacem's services to pay. Now he wanted his commission up front, even before a flock of suppliers involved in the construction of an oil terminal on the east coast had paid Sacem. The prince sent a messenger to state that unless Keith Carmichael paid up immediately, Sigma would pull out of the co-operation agreement. The obvious consequence would be that his company would have to withdraw from Saudi Arabia while he risked being thrown into jail, the Prince's messenger hastened to add.

That autumn, Keith Carmichael had spent the best part of five years in Saudi Arabia. He knew a heavy hint when he heard one. And he knew the kingdom well enough not to dare counting on the understanding of the Trade Ministry's Trade Dispute Settlement Commission.

Keith Carmichael made the best of the dusk prayer hour to sneak his Nissan through a dry river bed, past two Saudi border posts and into Qatar – to a feeling of freedom that was as exhilarating as it was brief. He was arrested even before he could reach the British representation in the country. A couple of days later, and without having had the opportunity to call his embassy, he was handed over at the border to the Saudi police.

It could have cost him his life, and it was close to costing him the use of his limbs. In Riyadh he was thrown into one of the tiny cells known as the 'dog kennel' at the special security prison where Saudi Arabia puts its political prisoners. The light was left on 24 hours a day, the steel door was opened and slammed with an infernal noise and he was forced to use the same floor he slept on as an open lavatory. During the day the temperature rapidly climbed to over 45°C (110°F).

When one day he refused to allow himself to be raped by one of his guards, the more direct torture began. At that time he still had not heard the charges against him, nor seen a lawyer and nor received a visit. He had not been allowed to call his embassy – the representative of one of the countries which, together with the USA, had been responsible for the development of the kingdom's state-of-the art armed forces.

One of his torturers was frank enough to tell him that he had been trained at a US military academy. He was placed in British-made handcuffs and fetters and exposed to one of the favourite methods of torture in the Middle East: falaka, that is whipping of the soles of the feet, which after a while start to crack, bleed profusely, then swell. Day after day he was asked to sign contrived charges of fraud against the royal family and the government and illegal entry into a military area. However tempting it may have been to sign in the hope of escaping further torture, such admission could have resulted in a punishment far worse.

Carmichael held fast, and so did his torturers. From time to time they threatened him with their close relationship with Prince Saud. Around Christmas time, they came up with new charges mixed with threats of even more abominable torture and endless years in a Saudi Arabian prison.

It was not until 84 days had passed, without his seeing a judge, a lawyer or an official indictment, that he was transferred to the Civil Rights Centre in Riyadh, where more than 30 prisoners often share a cell built for eight. After a few days, vice-consul Richard Northern came to visit. At that time Keith Carmichael was pretty broken man. His feet were in a terrible state, his weight had fallen by a third, his body dehydrated in the extreme and his kidneys failing.

The British Embassy, however, had what it considered more pressing problems to deal with. Britain and Saudi Arabia had just been through two years of crisis, first the murder of a British nurse in Riyadh, then a sensational BBC documentary about the execution of a Saudi princess for adultery. The film showing the shooting of the princess and the decapitation of her lover in the street had made an outcry in Britain. The relationship between the two nations had been at its lowest ebb and the British ambassador was in the process of rebuilding sensitive links. The last thing he needed right then was a British torture victim behind Saudi bars. Incredibly, vice-consul Northern urged the suffering Keith Carmichael to keep a low profile.

On several Fridays, a very special sergeant turned up in the cell. The other prisoners knew and feared him. He came without warning, but every time with the same purpose – to pick out and take away a prisoner for execution on the square after Friday prayers. Many of the prisoners only had stumps left where the kingdom's executioners had taken a hand or a foot. In the meantime the charges against Keith Carmichael mounted. But he was allowed to receive visits from those old acquaintances who dared risk their own security by acknowledging their friendship with him.

To begin with he counted the days; then the weeks. But months seemed to hurtle by. It was not until May 1982, nine months after his arrest, that he managed to write a letter of complaint about his torture. He had a copy delivered to his embassy. At the same time he made sure that the message got out of the country to influential friends in Britain and the USA, where his case was finally brought to the notice of the authorities. As spring arrived in Europe, the temperature in Carmichael's cell increased, topping at over 50°C. His health deteriorated rapidly.

He was moved about between various prisons in Riyadh, where he shared cells with a few foreigners, but mainly with Saudis arrested for doing the same as his friends in the upper echelons of society – drinking alcohol. Time moved on, while his health deteriorated still further. At times he was so unwell that the Saudi prison authorities had him examined by a doctor; always in handcuffs and frequently fettered.

During one transport from the prison to hospital things nearly went very wrong. The drivers always enjoyed the special pleasure of putting their foot down over the bumpiest bits of the road so that the prisoners packed into the back of the lorry were thrown from side to side and up and down between the iron girders in the floor and roof. One day, Carmichael was thrown off balance so that his back was smashed against a sharp metal edge. He screamed out in pain. His guards retorted with blows and kicks to his ribs when he could not get out of the Toyota Landcruiser on his own. One of his vertebrae was damaged. He was put into a sort of corset and left chained to a bed.

The first large-scale article about the Keith Carmichael Affair appeared in the *Daily Mail* on 19 August 1982, 10 months after he had attempted to flee Saudi Arabia. The former British company director and friend of members of the Saudi royal family was now a handicapped wretch on the verge of death, emaciated and exhausted. Increasing international interest in this Westerner, perhaps linked to the Saudi authorities' fear that their prisoner might die at the hands of brutal jailers – the recipe for a diplomatic problem – was probably the reason for a Committee of Inquiry suddenly being set up to evaluate his claims of having been tortured.

Carmichael was in a bad state, still ready to fight his oppressors. He pointed out the jailers who had tortured him. Back home in London, one of his old friends from one of the clubs, deputy foreign minister Douglas Hurd was asked on the BBC's lunchtime news broadcast 'The World at One' whether Carmichael had been tortured. 'No,' the deputy minister replied. He did not believe they had.

Time passed, but one day a message arrived from the palace that Keith Carmichael was to be treated at the Saudi Arabian forces own hospital, where he was taken handcuffed and fettered. A Swedish physician, Dr Tillberg, received him and with considerable courage demanded that his fetters and handcuffs be removed. He was quickly able to establish that the same patient whom Douglas Hurd had found in a reasonable condition, had a damaged vertebra and was also suffering from malnutrition, dehydration, low blood pressure, and wasted muscles as a result of his detention. A report from vice-consul Northern claimed, according to *The Observer* newspaper, that Carmichael had said he 'felt quite well and had not been troubled with any kind of medical problems'.

He was soon back at the Civil Rights Centre, in his old stinking dirty prison cell, where yet another Briton had been incarcerated. This 'colleague', however, was released after six months, without ever being charged with anything. Carmichael then decided to go on hunger strike, despite the fact that visitors and fellow inmates warned him that his health would not stand any long-term attempt to force his release in that way. The deputy governor of the prison declared that nothing could trouble him less than Carmichael's death. But when, after three weeks, Carmichael was suffering severe giddiness and was in terrible pain, he was brought before this very same deputy governor who had a visit from Richard Northern's consular replacement. Both urged him to abandon his hunger strike, but Carmichael refused.

At the security forces' hospital, the Swede Dr Tillberg had been replaced by Dr Bettendorf of Luxembourg, who helped to draft a declaration of Keith Carmichael's illness. With the help of a visitor this was quickly forwarded to Amnesty International and several other human rights organisations and created a storm in the press. In Riyadh, the new consul, Boardman, said he regretted that Carmichael had troubled the Saudi authorities! The prison's deputy governor, on the other hand, promised that Carmichael's case would be rushed through if only he would be so kind as to eat. Carmichael took solid nourishment for the first time in 30 days.

In January 1984, after two years and three months in prison, torture and illness, the governor of Riyadh declared to the British ambassador that the whole affair had been a 'mistake'. But Keith Carmichael had to wait a further two months before his gaoler woke him on 17 March 1984 with the message that King Fahad, who had inherited the throne while Carmichael was in prison, wanted him set free. The deputy governor invited him to dinner in his own home in Riyadh. Carmichael was free to go home.

Nobody could give Keith Carmichael back his health and certainly not the two years and three months during which he had confronted evil itself. To this very day, he suffers pain from his period in the Saud family's jails. He no longer presides over an international business concern but over 'Redress', a small but highly respected charity which helps torture survivors obtain reparations. Today he knows that he was far from alone in his experience of the abuse of power in Saudi Arabia. He has met some of the others, such as US systems operator Scott Nelson who was arrested because he pointed out problems of poor maintenance at the King Faisal Hospital. Torturers smashed one of his knees during a month-long stay in a torture centre, where they got him to sign an Arab-language confession, although he did not understand it and it never was translated. A US senator got him out. Or the second American, the language teacher Jim Smrkovski, who worked for the Saudi airline, Saudia. He was imprisoned and tortured for 15 months before being convicted of alleged alcohol smuggling and thrown out of the country. During his time in prison they had kept him in a 'dog kennel' and pulled out six of his toe nails. He was helped to freedom by, among others, senator Bob Dole. Keith Carmichael meet the two of them during a hearing in the House of Representatives in Washington in May 1992.

They have one problem in common, which they are trying hard to get friends of the Saud family – the governments in Britain and USA – to take seriously. Each of them came to Saudi Arabia on a Western contract with the Saudi authorities, and each of them was abused by Saudi torturers. But as Amnesty International wrote in a report in 1996, 'not one single instance of reported torture, maltreatment or death during arrest has been publicly and independently investigated by the Saudi authorities'. There has certainly been no lack of requests on the part of Amnesty, Human Rights Watch and others. But the Saudi authorities have flatly denied every single allegation of torture.

How can one make Saudi Arabia accept its responsibility? It does not allow visits by international human rights organisations. It has not committed itself to the UN human rights system. It does not even allow local Saudi lawyers to investigate Saudi jails and the blood on the hands of their employees. Nor does it allow diplomats, not even those from the USA and Great Britain, to look into the prisons of the Interior Ministry.

Keith Carmichael and the others were faced with the problem that neither US nor British law provides for holding the torturers or their Saudi employers responsible at a court in the USA or Britain. Diplomatic immunity sees to that by enveloping and protecting the embassies.

But Keith Carmichael's US lawyer, Leonard Garment drew up another proposal intended to ensure that no country can withdraw from the international legal system. His proposal got as far as the approval stage in Congress, but was then stopped by the State Department and the White House. The idea was quite simple, and dignified, albeit politically hyper-sensitive. If it is not possible to obtain acknowledgement of responsibility for torture in the country where it took place, it must be possible to sue the state concerned in a US court. It would not provide a direct means of forcing an individual torturer before a court, but it could put the international spotlight on states and governments, responsible for torture. A majority was assembled in both the Senate and the House of Representatives in favour of the proposal in 1996.

It is actually based on a principle, which the US representative at the UN Human Rights Commission in Geneva has referred to as the most effective form of pressure. Shedding light on and exposing crime is precisely what dictatorships do not like, although they keep the lights in the cells of their victims burning day and night.

But shedding light on the darkest side of good friends was more than the US government could take. The State Department sent the proposal back where it had come from with the message that the administration would only accept that kind of proceedings against states that were already on the USA's list of governments behind international terrorism. This would make it possible to sue a number of Middle Eastern and North African representations such as the Syrian, Libyan, Sudanese, Iraqi and Iranian embassies – but with the notable exception of those of Saudi Arabia's.

But why that particular formulation? why precisely that choice of countries by the State Department? Leonard

Garment can see no other explanation than the foreign service's eternal fear of affecting the stability of relations with client nations – and the desire to remain on a good footing with a major buyer of weapons, aircraft and other technology.

In Keith Carmichael's ears, it rings like an echo of what the British consul in Riyadh had told him, 'Remember, we need the Saudis more than they need us.'

CHAPTER TEN

Just Allies

Never friends

He is bugged at home and unappreciated in the bazaar. He never gets used to it. Let's call him Philip. That is one of his conditions if he is to talk. 'Never use the phone and never call me by my real name,' he says during a visit somewhere in Europe. Instead, he gives me a fax number at a 'safe office' in Riyadh.

Sometimes he feels as though he is going insane. Strictly speaking, he is in Riyadh on behalf of a Western government which during the Gulf War demonstrated, with the blood of its soldiers, that it is Saudi Arabia's faithful friend. Even so, he and the people at his embassy are convinced that they are being bugged, both at work and at home. The phone is no longer anything more than a practical message system and even the evening meal with the wife has changed character. They chat in code as soon as the subject has anything to do with the state of power in Saudi Arabia. Perhaps this is not necessary all the time, but the fear of being bugged is just as effective as the most officious censor. Instead, the married couples go for a walk when they need a breath of fresh air.

At the embassy they have a U-boat, a bug-free room, where the ambassador and his staff can talk in peace about their friends in Saudi Arabia. 'It's just like it was in the Soviet era,' says Philip, 'The only difference being that here we are supposed to be among friends.'

◆◆◆

Riyadh, six months earlier. November 1995. A light commercial vehicle loaded with explosives is detonated outside the training centre of the National Guard, where US experts are helping to train the Saud family's special security force. Five Americans are killed, as are two Indians who happened to be in the wrong place at the wrong time.

For the USA it was an ugly warning of an even more bloody attack to come. On 25 June 1996 a larger truck blew up in front of an apartment block in Dhahran, in eastern Saudi Arabia, where US troops were accommodated. The entire front of the building was ripped off, 19 young Americans lost their lives. The USA went into shock. This did not happen during a war in enemy territory, but in a country the USA went to war to defend five years previously.

In fact, the Saudi authorities had in the meantime arrested, jailed and condemned four Saudi Arabians for the first attack. US agents asked to be allowed to interrogate them, but the Saud family saw fit to have them beheaded. The US agents returned home frustrated about a co-operation they did not understand.

Matters did not improve after the second bombing. 'They tell us nothing of significance,' explains one diplomat at the State Department.

The two bombings gave the Americans in Riyadh an unpleasant feeling of being unwelcome. They are used to being harassed by the authorities, but the bombs could only be a greeting from an opposition even keener to see the Americans well beyond the horizon.

They stayed out there before. During the 1980s, the US Navy was on the other side of the Straits of Hormuz, in the Indian Ocean, ready to protect Saudi Arabia and secure oil traffic on its way out through the Gulf, which to an alarming extent was being drawn into the war between Iran and Iraq. The war had been started by Saddam Hussein, who was also the first to let oil traffic suffer as a result. But those were different times; Saudi Arabia financed Saddam Hussein's war effort to a large degree, giving Iraq, among other things, 1,500 large US-supplied bombs – without consulting Washington. Even so, the USA stepped in as a guarantor against the escapades of the Iranians, not of Iraq.

After the second Gulf War in 1991 is was difficult to pretend that the Saud family was not being protected by and dependent on the USA. In all, 6,000 US soldiers, training facilities and planes were stationed on a permanent basis in Saudi Arabia, the vast majority of them in the eastern province which was already used to a lot of foreigners in the oil industry. More than 30,000 US civilians were working in the country in 1996.

However, for the Saudi opposition, not least the religious segment of it, this was tangible evidence of the Saud dynasty's alliance with heretical Westerners, a fact that wasn't seen to bring any good to Saudi Arabia.

Once in a while the US and British embassies were given a tip-off about new terrorist threats. In Washington, the administration therefore decided to label its partner, Saudi Arabia, a crisis area. Spouses and children were encouraged to go home.

Not a bad decision, perhaps. The Americans were not popular, unappreciated by the authorities, and hated by the radical opposition. What choice was there for American families in Saudi Arabia. The US and the royal family together decided to move the US soldiers out of Dhahran to a more covert base in the south of Riyadh.

At the same time, the US intelligence agency, the CIA, decided to carry out an evaluation of the crisis, to discover what was going on behind the scenes in the Gulf state. Saudi Arabia is 'one big black hole' when it comes to intelligence, one senior official told the *New York Times*. And if there is one thing the US does not want, that is to be surprised by revolutionary developments in Saudi Arabia like those when Ayatollah Khomeini effectively ousted Shah Reza Pahlavi in 1979.

The US did not want to see an anti-American development in Riyadh – not just because one-quarter of the world's oil is to be found in Saudi Arabia's underground. As time has passed, the concentration of weapons in Saudi Arabia and the lucrative arms market certainly has increased the American interest in Saudi stability. Between 1985 and 1994, the Saud family bought arms and military technology worth 38 billion dollars, making it the influential US arms industry's biggest customer. This is the case even though US law on international assistance demands that security assistance should not be afforded to 'any country, the government of which is involved in a systematic pattern of serious violations of internationally recognized human rights' (Foreign Assistance Act, Section 502B).

Mohammed Khilewi, First Secretary at Saudi Arabia's UN embassy in New York until he defected in 1994, says that during the same period the Riyadh government supported Pakistan's and Iraq's attempts to build a nuclear bomb.

According to the reputable *Jane's Intelligence Review,* it is doubtful whether Saudi Arabia would be able to make use of all its military shopping. The population still is small in relation to the size of its territory and the size of the armed forces will not increase significantly more than to the current 150,000 men, including reservists, since the Saud family, as an understandable exception will not import the necessary manpower for this purpose. Iran can put up 530,000 men and Iraq 430,000. But unlike these two countries, Saudi Arabia's rulers have no intention of introducing compulsory military service. One Western intelligence man finds it ridiculous that Saudi soldiers do not usually have access to ammunition. This demands permission from an extremely high-ranking figure in the military and the family.

Philip, our contact in Riyadh – whose name isn't Philip at all, and who could not be in Riyadh if the Saudi authorities knew that he spoke to government critics within the country and writers outside – speaks of 'strange bedfellows'. He naturally has no sympathy with people who drive trucks full of explosives into US camps, but his sympathy with the authorities he is posted in Riyadh to co-operate with is also limited. He says,

'It's playacting. One big play. Officially, we protect a religious, almost puritan kingdom. But the closer you get to it, the more hollow it seems. It is one thing to drink alcohol behind closed doors although it's illegal. But they drink, too, businessmen and princes and anyone with a bit of power, and the way alcohol is trafficked is so systematic that the princes have to protect, or even direct it. The same applies to videos, which are almost all people have to occupy themselves with in their free time as there are no cinemas or theatres. You can get practically anything you want on video, not with the proper box, but the tapes are all right. Everybody sees them, everybody knows they exist. But still they maintain the facade, the illusion of orthodoxy, while the princes, and others with power do precisely as they like. Pure hypocrisy.'

An office somewhere in New York. Autumn 1996. A Western diplomat with many years of service behind him in the Middle East, says,

'Of course we're in Saudi Arabia in our own interest and because Saudi Arabia has been threatened by Iraq and could be again, by Iran as well. But it becomes more and more pronounced that while we are only there to protect the country against outside aggression – the actual threat to Saudi Arabia comes from within. But then we can't do much about that.'

The dynasty is in a peculiar situation. It has the world's largest oil reserves and in the USA, the world's most powerful friend. During the Gulf War it had the support of 30 countries, willing to go to war for Saudi Arabia. It paid the bill for the war (almost 56 billion dollars according to *Jane's Defence*) in cash and initiated yet another round of military reinforcement. According to the IMF in Washington, it has reversed the poor economic developments of the 1980s. What is more, the dynasty has also secured itself the world's most convenient basic law. This gives His Majesty total power as both king, prime minister, supreme religious leader and chief of defence, securing the dynasty the sole right to rule in future. So what is the problem?

The people, quite simply. The people are the problem. For reasons the Saud family perhaps do not understand, perhaps do not want to understand, the people are not unequivocally enthusiastic and not willing for ever to do as the Saud family finds best. Not because the people agree for that reason on an alternative. But they do not even have the right to question the course the dynasty has set.

It may be that Saudi Arabians are uncertain about what is going on in the countless palaces the Saud dynasty has had built for itself. This is a problem for the dynasty's US partners as well. 'We simply know so infinitely little of what goes on in the inner circles of power – just as little as what is going on among those terrorists who threaten us with bombs,' says the diplomat. He believes there ought to be a difference; the Americans are after all in Riyadh to support the local government. But the government itself will not talk to the USA. And it does not allow other people to speak. It is distressed if American representatives visit Saudis who are critical of the regime. This actually happened when the US embassy in Riyadh contacted Mohammed al-Massari, the leader of the extremely critical 'Committee for the Defence of Legitimate Rights'. It only happened once. King Fahad demanded a written guarantee that the US would never talk to either al-Massari or others of his kind again. According to one source at the State Department, Fahad was given the answer that is was only quite normal and natural that the US keeps itself informed from all sides. However, al-Massari said in London in January 1997 that he had not been contacted by the Americans again since then.

A historic alliance is shaking. As far back as 1947, the USA promised to defend Saudi Arabia's territorial integrity and political independence. In 1950, Washington promised that it would act to defend Saudi Arabia if it were threatened by external aggressors – an assurance that was repeated by President Carter in the 1970s. He designated Saudi Arabia's security and stability in the Gulf as strategic priorities for the USA, a commitment confirmed by President Bush during the Gulf War.

At the State Department in Washington, however, diplomats who specialized in Saudi Arabia say point-blank that stability is under threat from within, not from without.

'We know some of the sources: for one there are the young men with an education but with no qualified work. Secondly religious people accuse the royal family of being corrupt and amoral. Thirdly, there is a risk that oil prices may fall once again making the regime unable to bribe the population with a state subsidised cushy life. But there are other sources of unrest that we cannot analyse: we simply do not know which way power inside the royal family will go after Fahad and Abdullah. We don't know whether the next generation in the royal family will be able to agree on a younger replacement or will accept the man who takes command and control. Nor do we know whether there will clerics, strong enough to protest openly. And we have no way of knowing whether members of the various armed forces would be willing to revolt.'

But the US continues in its partnership, as though nothing had changed, and in thus doing, it does not differ from Saudi Arabia's other partner, Great Britain.

'The unpleasant bit, seen from our observation post,' says a British analyst during the winter of 1996–97 in Whitehall, 'Is that on the face of it, it is difficult to see any threats – but the royal family is acting as though it feels unsecure. This ought to provide food for thought.'

Again, perhaps the problem is 'the people'. It is not unthinkable that the dynasty, when it comes to the crunch, is unsettled by its own almightiness. And can Saudi Arabia's partners ignore repression among friends?

Philip, our man in Riyadh: 'The problem is precisely – who are our friends? A royal family that is out of step with world political developments? Or – also in our own interest because of the oil – is it the Saudi Arabian nation we want the best possible relationship with? Until now our government's have given priority to the royal family. Is this not only shortsighted but also mistaken?'

An American ambassador who has been involved for many years in the formulation of the USA's Middle East policy says, 'Remember that there is a difference between an important country and one with which we feel an affinity. Saudi Arabia is important, but we will never sympathise with the values of the Saud family.'

Although people at the State Department are not keen to talk about it, Saudi Arabia's royal family measures up to most of the USA's and the West's worst conceptions of 'fundamentalism'. The Riyadh dynasty has created a society based on ancient religious scripts without contemporary interpretation. This society is administered in concert with government-controlled clerics with no common legal basis; with legal discrimination between men and women; with statutory differentiation between ruler and subject, dictated at the umbilical cord and (alleged) religious legitimatisation of medieval punishment, even though Muslims are the ones most hard-hit by the dynasty's policies. All the same, the rulers of Saudi Arabia are the West's most appreciated 'fundamentalists'. 'There is one decisive difference between the Saudis' fundamentalism and that of others,' says one diplomat at the State Department. 'Saudi Arabia is kindly disposed towards us, at least as far as security policy goes. And the others are not.'

◆◆◆

A shudder ran through both the Western and the Arab world when Ayatollah Khomeini came to power in Iran in 1979 and the world was no less apprehensive in 1992, when the 'Islamic Salvation Front', FIS, were on the verge of winning the free elections in Algeria. Both Western and Arab governments were so horrified that the two cultures shared the same point of view – rather a military coup and a junta than letting the citizens of Algeria choose a religious government of their own free will.

The governments of the West were ostensibly frightened that the election in Algeria would be the start of a religious dictatorship like the one in Iran. The Arab governments' greatest fear was that a FIS victory would inspire other religious movements – other 'fundamentalists' with an appetite for power and influence. However, both the Western governments and the Arab world had shown that they could live with dictatorships. The West had enjoyed a perfectly good relationship with Khomeini's predecessor, Shah Reza Pahlavi and most Arab states lived, then as now, under dictatorships. Numerous of them are among the USA's, Britain's and France's closest partners. So the problem in Iran and Algeria was not the prospect of a new dictatorship, but that of a spreading popular anti-Western uprising that could threaten existing stability.

It was more a question of power than of the use or abuse of religion. After all, the Saudi kingdom so far has been one of the most stable societies in the Middle East (with the same family in power since 1932) though dominated by what the West calls 'fundamentalism'. Saudi Arabia is a friend.

Two of the dynasty's assets have been useful to the Western world and governments of the Arab world alike: wealth and stability. For decades these two advantages have been seen as one and the same thing – as though the royal power itself were the key to oil and stability. This is the dogma that the Saudi dynasty will go to great lengths to perpetuate. The dynasty can depend on the West so long as it appears that any form of political upheaval in Riyadh would be ruinous to oil production and thus to the international energy system. New large energy producers in Central Asia will not be in a position to make the world less dependent on the steady flow of black gold from the Arabian Peninsular for another 10 to 20 years.

But even at the State Department they are asking the question: are the Saudis right, or would the oil flow regardless of who was in power in Riyadh? It is hardly plausible that any government in Saudi Arabia would be able to afford the alternative. Oil is the only certainty there is. Not stability; nor power in Riyadh.

'Saudology'

Portrait of a partner

Richard Murphy recognises the rumblings that accompany the distribution of a fresh new issue of the State Department's yearbook on human rights every winter. He has served as ambassador in the Middle East and as Deputy Secretary of State. He says, 'Countries like Saudi Arabia pretend they don't care but believe me, their diplomats queue up every year to find out how they have fared.'

For a Saudi Arabian diplomat bringing the report home cannot be a favourite task; it must burn his hands. It could be called a debilitating indictment from the courtrooms of global conscience.

> Page one: 'The government [in Saudi Arabia] commits and tolerates serious human rights abuses. There is no mechanism for citizens to change their government, and citizens do not have this right.'

'Believe me. This book does not make the work of a diplomat in Riyadh any easier', says one American who has served in the city. 'Saudi Arabia's government simply cannot understand how we can publish this kind of book about one of our partners.'

'There were credible reports that the authorities continue to abuse detainees, including citizens and foreigners. Ministry of Interior officers are responsible for most incidents of abuse, which can include beatings and the deprivation of sleep during weeks of interrogation resulting in severe weight loss for the detainee.'

It was not the State Department's initiative to publish the annual report on the human rights progress, but rather the Congress who require an accurate picture of the international situation ahead of decisions on US foreign policy.

'Efforts to confirm or discount reports of worse abuses, including torture, are hindered by the Government's refusal to grant members of diplomatic missions access to the Ministry of Interior detention facilities or allow members of international human rights groups into the country.'

Every country in the world is closely investigated. Every year it follows the same pattern, using the same criteria for law and order – those defined by the international community at the UN. In the ministry, I try to find out how the State Department expects Saudi Arabia to react to this book. 'No comment' is the answer (in Autumn 1996) from the office responsible for preparing the book for publication. 'No comment' says the Middle East office that deals with Saudi Arabia.

Richard Murphy, who sits at the head of a think tank in New York, provides us with the following guarded reply 'the report has integrity, all the details are controlled and assessed'. However, as everywhere in 'Saudology', there is no queue of people wanting to comment on the situation. It is similar to the 'Kremlogy' of the Cold War, the study of the closed system in the capital of the former Soviet Union. Nobody really knows exactly what goes on in Saudi Arabia or where the final decisions are made. No public body is involved in the process and the public is denied access.

No one knew the nature of the discussions that went on in the Politburo during the cold war, just as no one is allowed to listen in when the Sauds today meet for a family dinner. Instead, the population of Saudi Arabia, the foreign ambassadors and the international press – exactly as it was in Moscow – are now obliged to try to interpret the signals sent out by the powers that be. Who is the subject of today's photograph? Who is sitting closest to the King? Who is the first to be named in the TV news? Who been absent for the longest period? Meanwhile, rumours begin to circulate – and nothing feeds rumours so efficiently as closed systems.

A rumour was spread about King Fahad, who fell ill in the winter of 1996/97 and temporarily handed over control of the country to Crown Prince Abdullah. According to the rumour, Fahad had woken up in a taxi on its way to a royal aircraft bound for Spain. It is suggested that he was the victim of a conspiracy that wanted him out of the country once and for all. He might have spent the rest of his days in Spain just like his heretical big brother King Saud who in 1964, was forced to hand over the throne to his brothers and in 1969 suffered an ignominious death in exile in Greece. Whatever happened, Fahad suddenly appeared on the throne again, but there is many a Saudi Arabian who would love to have overheard the exchange of words between the Saud family's most influential brothers at Fahad's sickbed.

A fascinating story some would say, others would find it frightening. These family meetings control the destiny of an entire country, the daily lives of roughly 18 million people and the exchange rate of the world's fourth largest oil producer, and they are always held behind closed doors. The royal family members are born into power and have papers to prove that they do not need to give it up at any time. One of them is a king and – as long as the most powerful members of the family allow him to stay – he has the army, the government and the priesthood under him.

> 'The Government detain without charge people who publicly criticize the Government, or they charge them with attempting to destabilize the Government.'

A reasonably high-ranking diplomat from the State Department claims that everything in the yearbook is written by the US Embassy in Riyadh; 'we do not wish to interpret this', he adds. 'But we keep trying anyway.' Has he read how the two historical rivals, the neighbouring countries Saudi Arabia and Yemen are portrayed in the yearbook? The one country, USA's Saudi Arabian ally, is exposed as being a true-blue dictatorship while the poverty-stricken and frequently ostracized Yemen is attributed a series of sincere attempts to modernize its system of government. Is this in accord with the USA's foreign policy in relation to the two countries? 'Maybe not', he says, 'but it reveals an outstanding honesty in the yearbook of human rights.'

> 'In general, members of the royal family, and other powerful families, are not subject to the same rule of law as ordinary citizens. For example, judges do not have the power to issue a warrant summoning any member of the royal family.'

But does Saudi Arabia concern itself with criticism from the international community? Patrick Foster – the English businessman who experienced a Saudi Arabian prison from the inside – was always released from his ankle chains if a British diplomat came to visit him.

'Systematic discrimination based on sex and religion are built into the law.'

The statement looks definitive, as if the law can justify injustice.

'Foreign embassies receive many reports that employers abuse foreign women working as domestic servants. Embassies of countries with large domestic servant populations maintain safe houses to which citizens may flee to escape work situations that include forced confinement, withholding of food, beating and other physical abuse, and rape . . . Few employers have been punished for such abuse.'

Should we believe the diplomat from the State Department who is willing to talk as long as he is promised anonymity? Is the restrained and sober style of the American Embassy in Riyadh a deliberate attempt to play down the situation? 'If there were more palatable facts to record, they would undoubtedly be included,' says he. Is the yearbook put out in the Embassy for foreign visitors to read? 'Doubtful. People asking for the book will be given it to read but quite frankly, I don't think many people ask and even fewer would appreciate being given a copy to take home.' Who reads it? 'Congress. A few journalists. A few other embassies. To tell the truth we don't have our sights on a large circulation.'

'Freedom of religion does not exist. Islam is the official religion, and all citizens must be Muslims. The Government prohibits the practice of other religions.'

A Dane wanted to import a Christmas tree; this was strictly forbidden.

'Conversion by a Muslim to another religion is considered atheism. Public apostasy is a crime under Shari'a and punishable by death.'

There is nothing to talk about and nothing to discuss:

'The Government severely limits freedom of speech and the press. The authorities do not countenance criticism of Islam, the ruling family, or the Government.'

This is not a subversive statement from a revolutionary movement – merely a quotation from Saudi Arabia's most loyal friend.

Despite this, the highly respected Minnesota Advocates for Human Rights have accused the State Department for many years of showing unreasonable consideration for their Saudi allies. According to these lawyers, the report has omitted to comment on the most interesting occurrence in the kingdom, being the development of an organized opposition. The Minnesota Advocates have noticed a striking tendency in the report to create an image of a 'benign fundamentalism' from USA's important ally – the Saudi Arabian government – and one of a more 'dangerous fundamentalism' from the opposition. According to the Minnesota lawyers the only significant difference between the CDLR (the opposition's Committee for the Defence of Legal Rights) and the Saudi Arabian government is that the government supports the USA's foreign policy initiatives in the Middle East.

These same lawyers think that it fair to mention that it is the government and not the opposition that is responsible for the long list of human rights violations in the name of Islam. These include: torture, physical abuse, discrimination against women, offences committed by the Muttawas, discrimination against Shia Muslims, executions for practising so-called witchcraft and for atheism.

Massari, refugee in Europe

'A dangerous man'

The Saudi Arabian regime is afraid of him. The British Government is afraid of him. But, Professor al-Massari is just a small man with greying hair and a penchant for waistcoats; he certainly does not look dangerous.

Perhaps they should have let him stay where he was – Riyadh's first Arab professor of physics, a dynamic teacher committed to his profession. Perhaps he was just a little too committed for both the Saud family and the British government and this is where the problems started. The Saud family did not dare to let him wander around freely since he was a conspicuous campaigner and always at the forefront of any movements for political reform. Neither did they dare throw the well-respected and well-known research scientist into prison and from what he has told, they also spared him the torture usually used on others in the same situation. In London, where the professor suddenly appeared as an applicant for political asylum, the British Government found themselves in somewhat of a dilemma. On the one hand, they were afraid that the anger of the Saudi Arabian regime would affect Saudi business in London and on the other hand, they were loath to deliver him into the hands of the Saud family's executioners.

If Professor Massari was a terrorist who planted bombs it would be easier to handle him but he is not; instead he uses words to plant the seeds of revolution.

Mohammed al-Massari is a man in his prime, highly intellectual, a wonderful sense of humour and god-fearing. He is a scientist by profession and dedicated to political reform; from a Saudi Arabian point of view, a bit of a grumbler. In 1992 along with many other intellectuals, he signed a document drawn up in defiance of the monarchy which demanded improvements in government leadership and greater accountability. The document was undoubtedly articulate and clearly written since Professor Massari is a man of careful and deliberate words. In Massari's opinion the royal family are corrupt, hysterical, amoral, undemocratic and completely unsuitable as representatives of Islam.

These criticisms are more than Saudi Arabia can take. So much so that Mohammed al-Massari is considered a criminal in his own country. Prior to 1993, he did manage to be elected spokesman for the newly formed movement CDLR, 'Committee for the Defence of Legitimate Rights.' He was then thrown into prison for six months. 'They beat me with bamboo canes and just a little under the soles of my feet, nothing much, I can't complain,' he recollects. After six months in prison he was released since the palace imagined he would now stop complaining about the Saud family. But they made a big mistake; the worst was yet to come. Mohammed al-Massari escaped out of Saudi Arabia into Yemen and then travelled to London, only to acquire a fax machine. He began bombarding private and public organizations in Saudi Arabia with messages from the CDLR accusing the regime of fraud. Every week hundreds of telefaxes were sent. In Riyadh the man was difficult to control; in London, control was impossible. It was now painfully apparent that the problem with Massari was not violent tendencies, but that he was a man of powerful words.

In this way, Massari has put both the Saudi Arabian regime and the British government to the test. In Riyadh the regime chose to imprison Massari and was then led to believe it would be expedient to release him. It came to regret this decision when having escaped from its cage, the bird flew over the border to Yemen. In London, the government tried to shirk its democratic responsibility by offering Massari a home on the distant sunny island of the Dominican Republic.

This was not such a generous offer as it may have appeared to the inhabitants of this island with its palm trees, coral reefs, charter companies and hotels. In fact if the truth be known, this was an attempt on the part of John Major's government to get rid of Massari.

In a statement by the Minister of Home Affairs, Ann Widdecombe, it was said that the government had been 'approached' by Riyadh and 'representatives of British trade and industry', both of whom were of the unanimous opinion that Professor Massari 'had a detrimental effect on our relations with Saudi Arabians'. Her statement to the British press read 'if people come to this country and make use of our hospitality to attack friendly powers with whom we have good diplomatic relations and good business connections, it puts us in a very difficult dilemma. In this case we have come to the conclusion that it is in the British interests to have him removed.' The message was loud and clear. This was a very difficult person; he must be removed to another part of the world if possible! The Dominican Republic had already declared its willingness to take Massari in exchange for financial assistance from London. Give a little, take a little.

Lord Avebury, the liberal chairman of the Parliamentary Human Rights Committee was shocked. The government 'has given in to blackmail'.

An event occurred which brought the matter to a head yet again. In London, the Tunisian Embassy issued a statement demanding that the exiled Tunisian leader, the 'fundamentalist' Rachid Ghannouchi, be put on an other aeroplane out of London. Ghannouchi had been given political asylum in London and like Massari had been presumptuous enough to campaign for free elections in his home country. This was another instance of a dictatorship complaining – and bitterly at that – about the asylum system used by a democratic society. In Tunisia they find it difficult to believe that a European capital is willing to shelter a wanted Arab dissident, a man whom they consider to be a terrorist. Saudi Arabia followed suit and the Tunisian regime enjoyed a brief moment of hope that 'their man', Rachid Ghannouchi as well be expelled from Great Britain.

Professor Massari complained against the proposal to deport him, as heard at a press conference in Westminster: 'that such an important country could have fallen so low. It is almost similar to a highly respected businessman, whose word is usually worth more than his signature, who suddenly renounces his reputation, his character and his dignity for a couple of drug dealers.' But he was not sent to the Dominican Republic.

He went to the courts to test the British government and seek justice. After careful consideration the British High Court decided that London's foreign visitor was right. However, perhaps the Government did have the law on its side in one way, in so far as Massari could legally be granted asylum in what is known as a ' third country'. In this case the obvious choice would be Yemen as this was the first country of refuge. However, Yemen was hardly safe and since the Court had enough evidence to believe that Saudi Arabia would send agents after Massari, it was concluded that the Dominican Republic was not a safe alternative either. In short, the British authorities were instructed to review the case. A month later Mohammed al-Massari was granted a four-year residence permit for the United Kingdom.

Quite a demonstration of law and right. An independent court of law had won a case against the shallow motives of a democratic government. Professor Massari wasted no time thanking and congratulating the British system in a message sent via his favourite mode of communication – the telefax.

It is now possible for Mohammed al-Massari to sit on an overstuffed sofa in a flat not far from Paddington Station and explain what the government in Riyadh are most afraid of hearing. His name is not on the door and the neighbours are unaware of who is talking on the other side of the wall, but Massari is used to such discretion from his time in Riyadh. All things considered it is Riyadh's emissaries he would most like to keep out of his life in London.

He has three volatile points of view that he aims to make known all over Saudi Arabia and ideally to Saudi Arabia's allies. He even casts aspersions on the Saud family's relationship to Islam ('drunkenness and debauchery') and he describes the *ulemas* – the leading body of Muslim priests – as tools of corruption in the service of the Saud family, ('non-Muslims with stupid opinions'). He is constantly pressing for free elections, the last thing the Saud family could imagine introducing in Saudi Arabia ('it is vital that the citizens take control of the government'). Wait a minute, we might say, if we start with the question of Islam – isn't it true that modern Saudi Arabia is based on an alliance between the Saud family and the priesthood?

Mohammed al-Massari has an answer: 'There can be no doubt that Abdel al-Aziz's only concern was to make sure that he was the one in power. And from the moment the family secured its power, the influence of the sheikhs began to diminish. Nowadays, the sheikhs have resigned themselves to the role of rubber stamp – an empty endorsement of the royal family's decisions.' Do they have a choice? Says Massari,

> 'Yes, I believe they do, but one of the problems is that from an historical point of view the present-day priest-hood are made up of not real scolars. They have been appointed as ulema by the regime but out of thousands of aspiring students the regime only promotes those who support it and only this group is granted the right to issue the *fatwah*.
>
> However, in the history of Islam the integrity of the ulema has always been measured according to their willingness to challenge the regime in power at the time. The more they opposed those in power, the more credibility they achieved in the eyes of the population. This is actually beginning to happen again among the younger sections of Saudi Arabia's priesthood. More and more of them now end up in prison and their credibility is thus increasing at the same rate. Many of them have been arrested and this weakens the government's posi-tion in the eyes of the people. However, it is the responsibility of the ulema, the reformers and the

intellectuals to demand that the government answers to the people and if the ulema are mere pawns of the government they will never be considered leaders of a society based on religion. They cannot be supported by any organization but they must adopt a supervisory role.'

It could be that the Saudi Arabian *ulema* have, behind closed doors, already criticised the regime. But that does not help, says Massari, unless they come forward, like him. Then they will gain the trust of the people. 'The people of Saudi Arabia are deeply interested in the matter,' he says, 'This is evident from the number of underground leaflets that are distributed in the bazaar and read everywhere. It is clear that there is a great demand for criticism – far more than the regime would ever dare permit.'

Massari continues:

'Most of the judges are narrow-minded and backward. Those who have served as priests and judges during the last 40 years or thereabouts, are so badly educated that their intellectual level is miserably low. This can be partially excused by the fact that most of them come from poor Bedouin families of which we cannot expect a high intellectual standard. Nevertheless, the government could have arranged courses and offered them a better education. It could have invited high ranking *ulema* from Egypt and sent our own priests abroad to study.

Due to the low intellectual standard our judges also suffer from xenophobia and at the same time, have not been presented with more challenging demands. Since the regime is itself backward and unable to take part in any significant discussion, a backward family has been faced with a backward-looking priesthood and this has resulted in a somewhat messy situation.

On the other hand, if one goes back 150 years in American history the legal situation was not much better. One could be hanged in five minutes. The difference is that in America public opinion existed. New media appeared which allowed for discussion, suggestions for improvements and the demand for elections. Slowly, progress developed in the right direction.

In our case nothing has managed to pull in the right direction. The ulema were given the impression that they were acting rightly even when they got things wrong and at the same time they were terrified of Western influence. Thus, they became suspicious of every suggestion for change, new procedures, lawful judicial proceedings, possibilities of appeal, control of the police, etc.'

Does Professor Massari consider these issues as Western or universal? He says,

'Quite the opposite, I find legal security rooted in Islam to a far greater degree than in the cultures of the West. However, if we're talking about procedures, then these values are still not built into our new legal customs. A good example is what is known in the USA as the "5th Amendment" that says that you are not obliged to say anything that could be held against you in court. Islam goes much further and gives you the right to withdraw your confession at any time, even after sentence has been pronounced, indeed right up your execution if necessary; you are also in your full right to take the case to trial again. However, in the Saudi Arabian courtrooms this is never put into practice.

Instead, it is xenophobia and anti-Western feelings that cause our priests and judges to refrain from using Islam's own value system.

Since it is the regime that claims to be Islamic and it is the most important priests who support the regime – either through treachery or fallacy – those subordinate to them do not oppose the regime. But these things take time as demonstrated in American history if we go right back to the early 1800s. At that point in history the normal course of events never included any voices raised in opposition to declare a law passed by Congress as invalid. It was when Judge Marshall first declared a law as unconstitutional that the door opened for a subsequent separation of the legislative and executive power. Up until then everyone was frightened.'

In Massari's opinion it takes a few courageous people to instigate progress or to change the course of a society's development. Once in Riyadh an acquaintance of his, a judge in the city, was taken off a case by the Ministry of Agriculture who insisted on using the ministry's own judges. 'No', said Massari, 'the role of the ministry's jurists can never be anything other than advisory, they are not appointed by a judge and should only be used in administrative cases.' Therefore, Massari urged his acquaintance to complain to the ministry. 'Who do you think I am – Judge Marshall in the USA?', was the friend's response. And in Massari's opinion that is exactly what he should have been. 'If you claim to be a true believer, you must insist upon your rights even if it means your death. At least you can expect a better life afterwards.' But his friend did not have the courage.

Massari himself is willing to accept the ulema as 'completely sincere'. However, 'the fact that the ulema is established by a government so corrupt and so un-Islamic means that the sentences pronounced are equally so.'

Massari is undaunted in his criticism of what he considers the immoral regime in Riyadh.

'Everyone in Saudi Arabia agrees that the royal family is corrupt and indulges in drunkenness and debauchery. The only reason why the family still manages to maintain a small amount of authority is that they still stand for law and order and the people are afraid of the alternative. Nobody in Saudi Arabia wants another Saddam Hussein or a new Nasser but there are only three members of the royal family who are respected for their god-fearing attitudes. Most of the family's palaces are dens of iniquity – ask anyone in Saudi Arabia and they will agree.'

We might be tempted to ask why there has been no open rebellion. As Massari comments,

'There are several reasons why and one of them is ethical. The nature of the Sunni Muslim traditions means that the problems at present are not severe enough to provoke open rebellion. Another reason is Saddam, who is no better but behaves in exactly the same way and in many cases a good deal worse. The rulers of Saudi Arabia live in their palaces and give half of their money to the Devil himself, but at least they leave people alone if they're not politically active, and they do not rape my wife. This is important because according to the rumours in Saudi Arabia, this is precisely how the military regimes in Egypt and Syria behave. Therefore, the attitude of the people in Saudi Arabia is, "OK let them behave like that in the palaces as long as they leave me in peace in my own home." At the same time they are told by the ulema that "if the royal family does misbehave, God will surely correct them".'

Fear also holds them back, says Massari. 'But even really brave people fail to protest. In this way there was perhaps a little truth in what Karl Marx said, that religion is the opium of the masses although it is not just true of religions but also of ideologies.'

Saudi Arabia's problem is that all power, both legal and military, is in the hands of one family and the system is set up to ensure that nobody can place themselves in opposition to the family. What does Mohammed al-Massari demand? Free elections with freely elected political parties, where the government has to answer for its actions. From time to time he is told that he is against Islam. 'Rubbish,' says Massari. In his opinion this is exactly what Islam is – a question of the legitimacy of power.

Massari's hosts in London allowed their own decision to deport him to be put to the test by a court of law. These same hosts, the British government, allowed the decision to be rectified by a court of law. The regime that claims to be his and Saudi Arabia's legal ruler has never dared to accept the responsibility for its actions. Wherein lies legitimacy? Mohammed al-Massari puts the question. A dangerous question from a feared man.

CHAPTER THIRTEEN

Censorship

Operation Desert Shield II

Thursday, 10 March 1994. The Saudi Council of Ministers assembled in Mecca. On the agenda: defence of the Kingdom.

Three years previously an international coalition had just secured Saudi Arabia's freedom and turfed Saddam Hussein's Iraqi troops out of Kuwait in the famous operation 'Desert Storm.' On this Thursday, the Council of Ministers had gathered in Mecca to defend the Kingdom against an entirely different threat. Not from Iraq, nor from Iran or another Gulf War. The Gulf War had already secured Saudi Arabia's borders against threats from without. On today's agenda was the Kingdom's desire to defend itself against an invasion from above, from intrusive signals from orbiting satellites.

The battle did not last long. The Saudi Council of Ministers decided to ban the import and sale of satellite dishes. This is how an autocratic dynasty defends its religious and moral values: law number 128 – all imports of satellite dishes are banned. On the other hand, the Saudi Ministry of Information would 'assume responsibility for the establishment of a system for the reception of foreign television signals . . . and to deliver them via a cable network to viewers in the Kingdom in harmony with its religious and social values.' The penalty for importing a dish and initiating one's own TV transmissions was set between 100,000 and 500,000 Riyals or between 26,000 and 133,000 American dollars.

Not a law that any police chief would be glad to enforce. The Gulf War itself had just tugged hard at the carpet under the royal Saudi censor. In the autumn of 1990, when hundreds of thousands of US troops flooded into new bases along the east coast, Saudi citizens had to seek cover from Iraqi Scud missiles. The war generated massive interest among Saudis as they followed events on television in their own living rooms. The first 20,000 dishes – nobody knows the exact number – were erected on rooftops throughout Saudi Arabia during the months of the war. Many thousands more were installed in the years after the desert storm over Kuwait had settled. The magazine *Middle East Economic Digest* estimated in its issue of 21 March 1994 that a total of 150,000 satellite dishes were providing a million people in Saudi Arabia with television signals at the time the government in Mecca decided to ban the equipment, while the *Financial Times* estimated the number of dishes at 400,000. In this respect, the Saudis resemble everyone else: they have a ferocious appetite for news and the entertainment that television brings right into their living rooms from every corner of the earth.

However, everyone from the King to his ministers and the regime's loyal priests were unsettled by the ungovernable flood of words and images of uncalibrated quantity and quality that suddenly flooded the airwaves. The Muttawas were extremely concerned by the immoral content of the programmes. The clergy was no less perturbed by the way satellite television insulted Saudi religious values. The dynasty was unaccustomed to the political pluralism which threatened to set an uncontrollable new agenda.

Western critics should think twice before exclaiming their disapproval at the ban on importing satellite dishes, wrote the editor of the newspaper *al-Hayat,* Jihad Khazen. He noted how the United States usually attacked countries like Iran for 'exporting its revolution', but according to Khazen, the US has its own habit of using its media to export what he considered to be undesirable characteristics to other countries, not least violence.

What was a dutiful Saudi police chief to do? The home is supposed to be inviolable in Saudi Arabia. Most dishes were invisible, hidden behind walls and balconies. But in June 1994 the Ministry of Domestic Affairs played its trump card. It now became illegal even to own a satellite dish. Citizens were given a month to sell their dishes abroad or they would incur a heavy fine.

The ink had barely dried on the government's new resolution when people started to move their dishes out of sight. On many roofs a new water tank suddenly appeared, hiding the offending dish. But the government was a step ahead. In future, a state-owned cable network – under the auspices of the Ministry of Information, would procure television for Saudi Arabian viewers. The ministry's only condition, was that stations who wanted their programming distributed on the cable network had to show due respect for the national interests and traditions of Saudi Arabia. The ministry, of course, would interpret and select.

◆◆◆

On the other side of the Persian-Arabian Gulf, another kind of modern technology helped to pave the way for a revolution in the Gulf's rival Great Power; the one taking place in Iran. While Ayatollah Khomeini was still in exile in Paris, his religious and political speeches were selling fast in the bazaars of Iran. Cassette tape-recordings meant that Khomeini's voice could be heard everywhere. The Shah's secret police did their best to trace and ban the tapes, but to no avail. The world saw its first Islamic revolution, popular in nature and helped on its way by a technology the former dictatorship was powerless to bridle.

The Saudi Arabian police offer rewards to citizens willing to inform on those responsible for the cassettes now flourishing in the Saudi market. In this case it is not the voice of Ayatollah Khomeini but frequently of other religious leaders who since the Gulf War have been circulating condemnations of amorality in the dynasty and the defilement of Saudi tradition. During the Gulf War the cassette tapes cautioned against leaving the defence of the realm to godless Western soldiers. Since the war, the same clerics and political circles have continued their campaign against the royal family's administration of power.

The tape cassettes are smuggled in, but there is another piece of technology that has extended the Saudi dynasty's dilemma: the telefax. It has become a natural tool for business, government and private communication in Saudi Arabia. But just as with the cassette tapes it depends who feeds the fax. In the 1970s and 1980s, the Saud family tried to control and regulate the number of typewriters and faxes by demanding possession of a licence for such potentially dangerous instruments, but by the end of the 1980s it was far too late. There were typewriters and fax machines everywhere. In London, the exile movement, the Committee for the Defence of

Legitimate Rights, bombarded the kingdom with faxed letters. Many hundreds of private and public addresses, including King Fahd's cabinet, received letters with 'alternative' news about the government, the royal family, about corruption and opposition calls for reform.

To ban fax machines would be as simple as banning sand on the Arabian Peninsular. Saudi Arabia is, after all, in the process of rapid commercial development, where communication, both internal and with the world outside, is not just desirable but necessary.

Certainly since the Gulf War, the dynasty has realised that technology, crucial to development, is difficult to control. Along the fax is the personal computer and the Internet with undreamed of quantities of information, which the Saud family would prefer to keep outside. An example is the London committee's fax series 'Prince of the Month', which has subjected members of the dynasty to humiliating polemic, exposing their debauched life and pursuits. The fax is more powerful than the sword, says the slogan from London; the Internet likewise.

In Riyadh, the Saudis have wasted no time getting onto the World Wide Web. It is true that the dynasty is trying to control the local servers and thereby those who access the Internet, but users simply log on via phone numbers in Great Britain or elsewhere in the West. The rest is easy. Information of all kinds, including criticism of the Saudi dynasty, is available on screen in Riyadh, Jidda, Dharan. The censor is powerless.

George Orwell saw the day of reckoning before him as he was writing into the future. But he came to the wrong conclusion regarding the technological control of dictatorships. It went the other way. Dictatorships make good use of the latest technology, including Saudi Arabia with its efficient phone tapping and bugging of private homes, companies, dissidents, mosques and foreign embassies. The technology itself is still without political colour, but its revolutionary potential is omnipresent. In Saudi Arabia, the Islamists in particular have adopted the new technology as a tool for the dissemination of its dynasty-critical message.

The new electronic signals are thundering into the 'Silent Kingdom', as Saudi Arabia was dubbed by the international freedom of speech movement 'Article 19' in London. But where might the noise to come from anyway? A long series of security laws and political rules consistently subdue or exclude undesirable noises – Political parties – forbidden; other political organizations – forbidden; trade unions – forbidden; strikes – forbidden; public criticism of government and ruling dynasty – forbidden. Newspapers and books are crudely censored (by the Ministry of Information). Imports of papers and books are usually censored by crossing out offensive photos and or text, in the most extreme cases papers and magazines are banned. Simple contact with a political organisation within the kingdom or without is also forbidden, as is providing others with offensive or critical information, graffiti or other methods of disseminating anti-government ideas.

The intelligence service 'al-Mabahith al-Amma' is responsible for control. The service can do exactly what it pleases as long as it is in the service of the dynasty. Citizens arrested for committing anti-state activities are sent to special prisons without being introduced to an 'ordinary' Saudi court of justice.

◆◆◆

The dynasty in Riyadh was the first to admit that new technology is not the problem, but how to use and control it – thus the ban on satellite dishes and the royal family's attempt to channel all satellite television through state-owned cables. In addition, the Saudis have purchased satellite transmitters to send television from Saudi Arabia to other Muslim societies.

On Friday 6 January 1995, the dynasty decided to put on a most peculiar satellite show. On that day at the King Fahad Stadium in Riyadh, 11 Saudi and 11 Mexican footballers kicked off on a pitch in the middle of the desert kingdom. Six winners of championships in the various continents of the world met in Riyadh to compete for the King Fahad Cup. But something was missing: the almost total lack of the supporters. The Saudi Arabian host team was the only one allowed to fill the grandstands with its own supporters in this land without tourism, inaccessible to soccer's international worshippers. The Danish team, who later won the cup, had to warn its residents in the kingdom beforehand not to wear the Danish flag, with its Christian cross, in the street. Inside the stadium, players of course wore shorts. Outside, the same attire would attract the attention and later the stick of the Muttawa, followed by arrest. A guide produced for the Danish players prior to the tournament said 'Avoid arrest. You will be considered guilty until proven innocent.'

The body language of football was transformed into TV theatre. Only the royal power's ban on foreign guests could explain why the stands were not full, even with the world's best team on the pitch. But the intention of Fahad's International Cup was to use satellite technology to transmit pictures of apparent cultural modernism to a world that was neither welcome nor could be tolerated in Riyadh, and to allow fans all over the world to receive the signals on the same dishes the dynasty forbids the use of at home.

Saudi Arabia is certainly not prepared to allow foreign satellite programmes to be broadcast, not even into the royally controlled cable network. This became clear a few months later, Thursday 4 April 1996, when the BBC's Arabic Service broadcast a rather sensational documentary in its *Panorama* series on the violation of human rights in Saudi Arabia. This proved to be a film to which the Ministry of Information took great exception.

The programme was carried to Saudi Arabia by a satellite owned by the Rome-based company Orbit Satellite Television. Orbit was owned by the Saudi company Mawarid, which in turn was owned by Prince Khalid, a cousin of King Fahad and married to His Majesty's sister.

Already in January of that year – at the expressed annoyance of the BBC – Orbit had blacked out a BBC report on the John Major government's decision to deport the Saudi exiled leader, Mohammed Massari, from London. This time Orbit did not simply make do with applying censorship. Instead, the BBC was informed that Orbit would no longer carry its Arabic Service. Of course, Saudi viewers were not consulted.

◆◆◆

To maintain an impermeable shield against outside satellite broadcasts requires money, power and physical control. But it is still a struggle the dynasty is doomed to lose. It is futile and impossible to try to check every cassette tape, to tap every single phone call and to manage all fax machines in the kingdom.

Satellite dishes are hidden behind water tanks and house walls throughout the land. They are also becoming smaller and ever better at receiving programmes clandestinely.

At a conference in January 1997 in Abu Dhabi, Saudi Arabia's tiny neighbour on the Gulf, a survey revealed that satellite TV is the chosen source of news in Saudi Arabia, not least from international news channels which refuse to allow themselves to be censored. Though it has tried, the dynasty has failed to keep new technology out.

CHAPTER FOURTEEN

Harry Wu

Double standards

Harry Wu was given special treatment the last time he was under arrest in China. He was only handcuffed on one occasion, when he was arrested in the summer of 1995. He was alone in his cell in Wuhan jail, apart from two guards. He was given the same food to eat as they, not the awful rations otherwise served to prisoners in Chinese labour camps where political prisoners are usually locked away.

Wu knows 12 of the camps from the inside – they stole 19 years of his life from 1960–79. Since then he returned to China three times on a US passport looking for documentary evidence of the corrupt labour camp system. In the summer of 1995, things went wrong at a rather awkward juncture for the Chinese powers just before the giant UN womens conference in Beijing.

They certainly did not need an international commotion to develop over a US citizen in a Chinese prison. They initially threatened him with execution, but instead opted for a 15-year gaol sentence and instant extradition.

What bothered Harry Wu most during his 66 days as a political prisoner was something more mundane: 'All the plainclothes police officers were carrying US Motorola phones. It is really troubling that US products are helping to make the Chinese system of repression more efficient,' he said.

Harry Wu has never been to Saudi Arabia, but he does know what human rights look like from the wrong side of a prison window. 'There is one thing dictators are more afraid of than anything else – i.e. noisy demands for respect for human rights. Every time it is mentioned in relation to co-operation with them it hurts.'

'But does it help to pressure dictatorships,' I asked one day in Washington, DC, when I meet him at the office of the American trade union AFL-CIO.

'That's why I got out so quickly this last time. They are dead scared of American pressure,' Wu replied. He has spent his whole life trying to get his new country, the United States of America, to take his old country, China, seriously. He studied geology and headed his university's baseball team in Shanghai when his life took a violent turn. Criticism of the Chinese communist party sent him straight into a labour camp as a 'counter-revolutionary'. He buried one of his friends in one camp and afterwards swore he would dedicate his life to fighting the Chinese gulag and the vicious system that cast human beings into prison because of their political beliefs.

The colour of the political system was different to that of Saudi Arabia, but the oppressors' impression of a right to persecute dissidents belongs in the same category. Both countries deny that the outside world has any right to interfere in their internal affairs. Neither of them offer citizens the right to fair, open trials or to the right to freedom of expression. The UN Human Rights Commission in Geneva has given both countries bad marks in the confidential 1503 hearings, but both boast considerable skills at keeping criticism at bay.

Universal rights? Do they exist, I ask. Harry Wu is familiar with the questions, but has never cared for it. He says,

'Sometimes people tell me that democracy will come to China together with capitalism, and that the best thing we do is to trade with China. That is a vicious lie. If it were true, why did they not recommend trade as the best instrument towards the Soviet Union. And why have they used arms embargoes against Cuba and Iraq? Why did they not do the exact opposite and recommend that we all trade with Castro and Saddam, making that lead to democracy . . . No, the problem is that some countries – like China and probably Saudi Arabia as well – are too big and too attractive as markets for our governments and companies to take democratic responsibilities. Pure double morals.'

'They also refer to the need for stability – but what kind of stability? Communist stability? Stability for the rulers of Saudi Arabia? It can't be the prisoners languishing in their jails who need stability, can it?'

Harry Wu continues,

'Other people tell me that democracy comes with development, when people get better off. That you need a middle class before you can consider demanding democratic reform. That's a grand lie, too. Try taking a walk in downtown New York City and look at the homeless, poverty-stricken people there. Would you tell them that they must first get some resources together, then they'll get their democratic rights?'

But isn't this all getting a bit too ethnocentric if we demand of China and Saudi Arabia and all others that they need the same kind of democracy as we have?, I ask.

Harry Wu replies:

'Britain, France and the US are all democracies although their styles differ, the electoral systems, their presidents, monarchies. But the content is the same – the same freedom, the same access to influence and to change of government. It may well be that democracy in Saudi Arabia and China will look even more different. But the fundamentals will be the same. Should the Chinese or the Saudis really have a different set of rights? Of course not. It might sound clever, but just you try telling someone in a tight spot that they have different, fewer rights – you simply can't do that.'

CHAPTER FIFTEEN

Defector in New York

From diplomat to refugee

Mohammed al-Khilewi resembles other refugees: he keeps looking over his shoulder, keeps an eye on uninvited guests, does not speak on the phone unless absolutely necessary and never with strangers. But he is elegantly dressed, his hands are beautifully manicured and Mohammed al-Khilewi still resembles the Saudi Arabian diplomat he no longer is.

His fate belongs to the accounts of the Cold War, among those courageous dissidents who were lucky to escape from the former Soviet Union or other dictatorships. Some of them hit the front pages of Western newspapers when they managed to give one of the many delegations to the West the slip – delegations that took the utmost care of their members. Or if they were exchanged for spies across the Iron Curtain of Europe in a thick morning fog.

Mohammed al-Khilewi is a dissident, himself, but unlike the Russian dissidents of the Cold War he did not escape from an enemy country, but from one of the USA's most important allies.

He is not exactly a beloved guest in the US, in fact one

the government in Washington DC would prefer to be left without. On 17 May 1994, 31 year-old Mohammed al-Khilewi, first secretary at the Saudi Arabian UN mission, made good a decision he had taken long ago. At that time he had assembled a dossier of some 14,000 documents related to corruption, repression and other crimes in Saudi Arabia. Khilewi was now prepared, as the first ever Saudi diplomat in the USA, to apply for political asylum.

But Khilewi did not want his move to be interpreted as simply running away. Before his escape he sent a cable to Crown Prince Abdallah and to his then superiors at the Washington DC embassy. In the cable he complained of widespread corruption in the kingdom, the repression of women, imprisonment of political dissidents, of unfair social conditions and the violation of human rights.

Within a matter of few hours, Khilewi explains, the Saudi ambassador, Bandar bin-Sultan, was on the phone, stating that he would send a private plane to pick up Khilewi in New York for an interview. When Khilewi hesitated, the ambassador quickly sent over one of the security people from the mission to persuade this presumptuous individual. The emissary forced his way right into Khilewi's bedroom and recommended that he go to Washington to finish his conversation with Sultan and that the life of his wife and three children could be in danger. Khilewi, however, preferred to go underground than to visit his Washington embassy.

His own predicament was acute, personal and potentially lethal. Washington's, though, was also considerable. Receiving Khilewi could be interpreted as a clear admission that repression does exist in a country which the US, only three years earlier, had dashed into war to defend. None the less, the US Immigration and Naturalisation Service called a spade a spade. In only 97 days

Khilewi was given political asylum with direct reference to the fact that he suffered 'well-founded fear of persecution on returning' to his homeland. The superpower had stood by its humanitarian principles. But it also stood by its own interests – which is why neither the immigration authorities nor the State Department in Washington wish to comment on Khilewi's defection and his fear of returning home.

The USA had taken in its first Saudi defector. He had already sent his dossier abroad as his own private life insurance, and unlike so many other of the world's refugees he does not have to worry about social problems. In New York, Khilewi moved about between different apartments so as to avoid 'friendly conversations' with the royal family's emissaries. His claims are neither few nor petty. The former diplomat – who has university degrees in political science and a diplomatic training behind him – allowed the *Sunday Times* newspaper to publish a document which ostensibly gives an account of a meeting between representatives of Saudi Arabia and Iraq in 1989. Khilewi was himself among the participants. The subject was Iraqi attempts to construct a nuclear weapon, financed with 5 billion dollars courtesy of the Saudi royal family. Khilewi also maintains that his dossier can prove Saudi finance of terrorist groups as well as massive violations of human rights in the kingdom.

A new human rights activist is born, albeit something of a lone wolf. Wise through bitter experience, perhaps, Khilewi is reluctant to rely on anyone, or to ally himself too strongly with anyone from the growing Saudi Arabian human rights network abroad. Who knows where the moles are? Who assists those they claim to be keeping a critical eye on? Many of his relatives back in Saudi Arabia are familiar with the shady side of Saudi prison walls.

This is why Khilewi has set his own course, although he has kept the CDLR (Committee for the Defence of Legitimate Rights) in London informed about his defection.

In a quiet restaurant not far from Manhattan in the winter of 1996/97, he was not ashamed of his ambition: 'To get the corrupt royal power in Riyadh replaced.' What makes him believe that this can be done? He replies,

'People in Saudi Arabia started questioning developments a long time ago, about the administration of power, the government – the decisions of the royal family, that is. They make comparisons with conditions abroad. And the opposition really made headway last year. People have begun to ask where all the money has gone. Since the early 1950s, billions of dollars have been spent on the military. The armed forces have actually consumed about 30 per cent of the national budget, but how was the money spent? When a few Iraqi troops came along we had to call on 30 nations to defend us. Where is the army? Where is the money? That these questions are being asked is the first sign that things will change. But note how most of the opposition believes in peaceful upheaval. Bloody upheaval might well be quicker, but the price would be too high.'

Where does Mohammed al-Khilewi find the opposition? In religious or more liberal circles, from the mosque or the liberal middle class?

Khilewi says, 'You can't distinguish like that, although this is common in the West. I consider myself to be a religious man. But it is probably right that many members of the religious opposition within Saudi Arabia have already been thrown into prison, while so-called Liberals generally are working in opposition abroad.

'There is a need for opposition at home and abroad,' says Khilewi.

'There is an awful lot that the CIA doesn't know or even want to know. For example, it occurs to me that the West doesn't want to know that none of the leading five people in Saudi Arabia has an education beyond the fifth grade. Well, the West has probably heard about this but nobody cares. Nor do they care when it comes to the democratisation of Saudi Arabia. They talk of a need for democracy in China or Iraq, but never in Saudi Arabia. They prefer to remember that Fahad was the country's first education minister, but prefer to forget that he was domestic affairs minister in the 1950s, when the regime murdered most of the opposition, including tribal leaders, supporters of the Egyptian leader Nasser, and so on.'

Do we have the same rights in Arabia and the West?

Khilewi answers, 'Of course, but the Saudi regime tries to use Islam as an argument of different rights. I don't understand why the West accepts this – as if a Bedouin, an Arab or a Muslim was not a human being with the same rights as everybody else.'

CHAPTER SIXTEEN

The Sting

Farewell to the king

The world over, royal families have had to yield to new rulers and in some countries to military regimes, but everywhere they are eventually succeeded by democracies and elected leaders when the time come. The only kingdoms that seem to be surviving are the constitutional monarchies, where the regent confines his – or her – activities to representing the realm, and allows the people to choose their own political leaders.

Several of them, kings and reigning queens alike, have been in Riyadh on official visits. They have walked down the guards of honour at Riyadh airport under a pavilion that is barely big enough to keep out the scorching heat of the Saudi sun. They have been received as guests at the extravagant palaces of the Saud family and experienced what royal rule once was like in their own part of the world.

On one occasion, one of these monarchs was set to leave for home. Fahad had invited the monarch to a banquet, and now it was the turn of the European to express a gratitude for a successful visit, during which several contracts had been signed, by returning the invitation at the European embassy. Fahad did not attend himself, but other members of the royal Saudi family appreciated taking part along with leading businessmen, people from the chamber of commerce and quiet a few diplomats.

In front of each plate stood four glasses, one for white wine, one for red and one for the sweet dessert wine as well as a glass for water. The red wine was particularly good, a chateau-bottled French claret. They made a toast to the friendship between two proud nations.

Outside was reality. Or was it inside? Events at the embassy were certainly routine. Servants from distant Asian lands served the wine and the four courses; some of the guests were Europeans in dark Western suits, others in Saudi Arabian *dishdashas*. The following day other guest workers made sure that the empty bottles were crushed into tiny fragments. The embassy concerned was well aware that powerful Saudis consumed alcohol in private – they were represented around that very table. Fahad had become so well acquainted with alcohol during the exploits of his youth in France and Spain that the family almost did not believe he was made of the right stuff to become king. The crushing of the bottles, however, was a facade, the upper class veil over a life that the Muttawas were punishing in the streets.

It was an evening like this, when Saudi Arabia was saying farewell to a monarch, that the Saudi king provided an aircraft to fly his guests home. A formidable storm delayed the party's departure. One of the roads from Riyadh to the airport was flooded by a rare thunderstorm.

Things were also pretty stormy in the film that was being shown – uncensored – in Fahad's plane. Who would forget *The Sting*, a lively comedy on gambling starring Paul Newman and Robert Redford as two petty swindlers who cheat a suitcase full of dollars out of a local Mafia boss on the American East Coast. They consume large quantities of alcohol, enjoy good fortune at the card table and have enlisted the help of the décolletée brothel mama 'Billie', who sleeps with one of them and makes sure the other one gets turned out as a smart gentleman, while simultaneously taking care of her brothel and her frolicsome girls.

In Riyadh's bazaar, the Europeans had experienced the Saudi Muttawas who, stick in hand, make sure that people attend prayers. In *The Sting*, the gambling, the prostitution and the alcohol have their own price and the Mafia boss his punishment. All this is censored and taboo in the land of the Saud dynasty, although members of the royal family have enjoyed it all in abundance. Gambling, sex and drink are all available at a price. But what members of the royal family indulge in is ruthlessly punished among ordinary citizens.

One day in the winter of 1996–97, rumour had it that Fahd was on his way to the airport where one of his aircraft was waiting. It was not in regular service, nor was it a special flight-of-honour for a monarch born to be king. It was more like a version of *The Sting*, a thank you and farewell from the family who, according to the rumour, wanted to say goodbye to one king and good day to another.

This kind of occupational hazard is difficult to insure oneself against. The Egyptian King Farouk was deposed in 1952, Libya's King Idris was toppled by a coup in 1969, the Shah of Iran in 1979. In between, Iraq waved goodbye to its royalty in 1958.

Safety is not even guaranteed within the royal family, as Fahad and Abdullah have always been aware, in as much as one of their elder brothers was deposed in 1964 and another, King Faisal, was murdered by a sick nephew in 1975. In neighbouring Qatar, the al-Thani emir experienced a similar fate, when a son exploited the ruler's absence abroad to take over power in 1995. After all, even the wise Sultan Qaboos of Oman came to power by deposing his father Sultan Said ibn Taimour.

So perhaps that was why Fahad, when one fine day he woke up in a car on his way to the airport, told the driver to return. For a frail king in Riyadh, with a lot of ambitious brothers and several thousand princes in his realm, a trip to the airport is not the best idea. One might just provoke a power struggle among members of the family back home.

On official departures, diplomats are always there taking note of the position of the princes in the line. For such are the terms of Saudology that power is interpreted through its symbols. Nobody ever has access to the place where the decisions are made – at the table of the Saud family.

Chronology

1720 – Saud bin Mohammad reigns as a local sheikh in central Arab Peninsular.

1745 – Mohammad, son of Saud, in alliance with preacher Abdul Wahhab, campaigns for religious piety and control.

1818 – Ottoman forces put an end to Saudi control. Great-grandson of Muhammad bin Saud killed.

1824 – Saud family takes back control of Riyadh.

1860s – Saud-family divided over succession.

1891 – Saud ruler, Abdul Rahman flees to Kuwait.

1902 – Abdul Aziz campaigns for control of Riyadh.

1912 – The brotherhood 'Ikhwan' established. Provides combat troops for Abdul Aziz.

1913 – Abdul Aziz takes control of Gulf Coast.

1925 – Abdul Aziz takes control of Mecca and Medina as well as all of Hejaz.

1920s – widespread rivalry and takeovers on the Arabian Peninsular.

1926 – Abdul Aziz ibn Saud becomes king of Hejaz and Najd.

1932 – Abdul Aziz ibn Saud establishes the Kingdom of Saudi Arabia under his own name.

1933 – Abdul Aziz appoints eldest son, Saud, as crown prince.

1938 – Oil is found.

1955 – Abdul Aziz dies. Saud takes over.

1958 – Faisal, younger brother of Saud, takes over executive power following family disagreements.

1960 – Saud retakes power.

1962 – Faisal promises to establish a consultative Shoura Council following family feud over calls from princes Talal, Badr and Fawwaz for greater liberality. Monarchy overthrown in neighbouring Yemen.

1964 – Following calls from members of royal family, the upper *Ulema* calls for change of power. Saud is followed by Faisal.

1969 – Saud dies in exile.

1973 – Arab-Israeli October War. Saudi Arabia backs oil embargo of the USA and others.

1975 – King Faisal assassinated by nephew. Followed by King Khaled. Prince Fahad becomes crown prince, side-stepping Saad and Nasir.

1979 – Shah deposed from Iran by popular revolution, led by ayatollah Khomeini. Sunni uprising in Grand Mosque in Mecca.

1980 – Iraq–Iran war.

1982 – King Khaled dies. His brother Fahad becomes king. Abdallah appointed crown prince.

1986 – Fahad decides to be 'the Custodian of the Two Holy Cities' instead of just 'Majesty'.

1987 – Riots in Mecca, instigated by pilgrims from Iran.

1988 – Saudi Arabia buys Chinese medium-range missiles able to reach Israel and Iranian capital Teheran; US protests; end of Gulf War.

1990 – Second Gulf War/ Iraq invades Kuwait 2 August.

1991 – US-led international forces liberates Kuwait. In Saudi Arabia King Fahad cancels old system of lifelong ministerial appointments and introduces four-year appointments.

1992 – King Fahad establishes a new consultative shoura by decree.

1993 – King Fahad appoints 60 members of new Shoura.

1994 – Widespread demonstration after arrest of religious radical Salman el-Ouda.

1995 – King Fahad acknowledges new emir of Qatar after his revolt against previous ruler, his father.

1995 – August; King Fahad replaces 16 ministers (finance, oil, information and others).

1995 – November; a car bomb in Riyadh kills seven people, among them five US advisers. Several movements claim responsibility.

1996 – April; four Saudi Arabian citizens are sentenced to death for the November 1995 bombing. US authorities refused permission to interview the group before public execution. In late June, another bomb kills 19 US servicemen in Dhahran. King Fahad seriously ill, Abdallah temporarily takes charge.

The Saud family: main line of succession

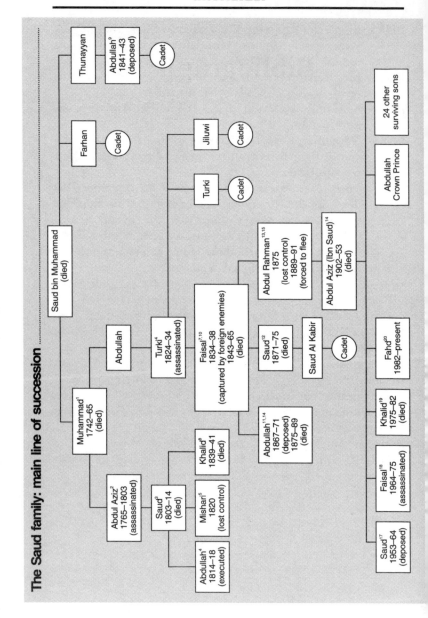

Bibliography

Abir, Mordechai, *Saudi Arabia, Government, Society and the Gulf*, Routledge, London, 1993.

Amirahmadi, Hooshang, *Oil at the Turn of the Twenty-first Century, Interplay of Market Forces and Politics*, The Emirates Center for Strategic Studies and Research, Abu Dhabi 1996.

Abureich, Saïd K., *The Rise, Corruption and Coming Fall of The House of Saud*, Bloomsbury, London, 1994.

Algosaibi, Ghazi A., *Arabian Essays*, KPI, London, 1982.

Almana, Mohammed, *Arabia Unified; A Portrait of Ibn Saud*, Hutchinson Benham, London, 1980.

American Community Services, *Welcome to Riyadh, Kingdom of Saudi Arabia*, Riyadh, 1993.

an-Naim, Abdullahi Ahmed, *Toward an Islamic Reformation: Civil Liberties, Human Rights and International Law*, Syracuse University Press, New York, 1990.

Article 19, Country Report. *Silent Kingdom: Freedom of Expression in Saudi Arabia*, London, 1991.

al-Azmi, Aziz, *Islam and Modernities*, Verso, London and New York, 1993.

Barber, Benjamin R., *Jihad vs. McWorld, How the Planet is Both Falling Apart and Coming Together and What this Means for Democracy*, Times Books, Random House, New York and Toronto, 1995.

de la Billiere, Sir Peter, *Looking for Trouble, SAS to Gulf Command*, Harper Collins, London, 1994.

Boulding, Elise, *Building Peace in the Middle East, Challenges for States and Civil Society*, Lynne Rienner, Boulder, Colorado and London, 1994.

Bulloch, John and Darwish, Adel, *Coming Water Wars in The Middle East*, Victor Gollancz, London, 1993.

Canadia Centre, International Pen, 'Freedom of Expression in the Muslim World, A Comparative Legal Studie of Blasphemy and Subversive Speech in International Human Rights Law and the Laws of the Muslim World', University of Toronto, Toronto, 1992.

CDLR (Committee for the Defense of Legitimate Rights), *Saudi Arabia, Financial Crisis and the Price of Oil*, CDRL, London, 1995.

CDLR, *Year Book, 1994–95*, A compilation of CDLR publications during its first year in exile, The Committee for the defence of Legitimate Rights, London, 1995.

Chubin, Chahram, and Tripp, Charles, 'Iran-Saudi-Arabia Relations and Regional Order, Iran and Saudi Arabia in the balance of power in the Gulf', Adelphi Paper 304, IISS, Oxford University Press, London, 1997.

Crystal, Jill. *Oil and politics in the Gulf, Rulers and Merchants in Kuwait and Qatar*, Cambridge University Press, Cambridge, 1995.

Dannreuther, Roland, *The Middle East in Transition*, IFS, Institut for Forsvarsstudier, Oslo, 1995.

Deegan, Heather, *The Middle East and Problems of Democracy*, Open University Press, Buckingham, 1993.

Dekmejian, R. Hrair, *Islam in Revolution, Fundamentalism in the Arab World*, Syracuse University Press, New York, 1995.

EIU (Economist Intelligence Unit), *Country Report: Saudi Arabia*, London, quarterly.

Field, Michael, *The Merchants, The Big Business Families of Saudi Arabia and the Gulf States*, Overlook Press, Woodstock New York, 1985.

Fried, Edward R., and Trezise, Philip H., *Oil Security, Reprospect and Prospect*, The Brookings Institution, Washington, DC, 1993.

Foreign and Commonwealth Office, Consular Department, *Living in Saudi Arabia, A Brief Guide*, London, 1994.

Fried, Edward R., and Trezise, Philip H., 'Oil Security, Retrospect and Prospect', The Brookings Institution, Washington, DC, 1993.

Fuller, Graham E. and Lesser, Ian O., *A Sense of Siege, The Geopolitics of Islam and the West*, Vestview Press, Boulder, Col. and Oxford, 1995.

Goldberg, Ellis, Resat Kasaba and Joel S. Migdal, *Rules and Rights, Democracy, Law, and Society*, University of Washington Press, Washington, DC, 1993.

Goodwin, Jan, *The Price of Honor, Muslim Women Lift the Veil of Silence on the Islamic World*, Plume and Penguin Books, New York and Harmondsworth, 1994.

Hallaba, Saadallah A.S., *Euro-Arab Dialogue*, Amana Books, Brattleboro, V, 1984.

Henderson, Simon, 'After King Fahad, Succession in Saudi Arabia', The Washington Institute Policy Papers, No. 37, Washington DC, 1994.

Hippler, Jochen and Lueg, Andrea, *The Next Threat, Western Perceptions of Islam*, Pluto Press, London, 1995.

Human Rights Watch, Middle East, 'Empty Reforms, Saudi Arabias New Basic Laws', New York, USA, 1992.

International Institute for Strategic Studies, *Strategic Survey 1995/96*, IISS, Oxford, 1996.

Ismael, Tareq Y., and Ismael, Jacquline S., *The Gulf War and the New World Order, International Relations of the Middle East*, University Press of Florida, Gainesville, Fla., 1994.

Khuri, Fuad I., *Imams and Emirs, State, Religion and Sects in Islam*, Saqi Books, London, 1990.

Lacey, Robert, *The Kingdom, Arabia and The House of Saud*, Avon, New York, 1991.

Lawyers Committee for Human Rights, *Islam and Justice, Debating the Future of Human Rights in the Middle East and North Africa*, New York, 1997.

Luciani, Giacomo (ed.), *The Arab State*, Routledge, London, 1990.

Macarthur, John R., *Second Front, Censorship and Propaganda in the Gulf War,* University of California Press, Berkeley, Cal., 1993.

McKey, *Saudis, Inside the Desert Kingdom,* Penguin, New York, 1987.

Mernissi, Fatima, *Islam and Democracy, Fear of the Modern World,* Virago Press, London, 1993.

Middle East Watch, *Empty Reforms, Saudi Arabia's New Basic Laws,* New York, 1992.

Minnesota Lawyers International Human Rights Commitee, *Shame in the House of Saud, Contempt for Human Rights in the Kingdom of Saudi Arabia,* Minnesota, Min., 1992.

Mohaddessin, Mohammad, *Islamic Fundamentalism, The New Global Threat,* Seven Locks Press, Washington, DC, 1993.

Morris International Associates, *Voice of the Arab World, Intelligence Report: Saudi Arabia, Its New Role in World Affairs,* London, 1993.

Munro, Alan, *An Arabian Affair, Politics and Diplomacy behind the Gulf War,* Brassey's, London and Washington, DC, 1996.

OPEC Bulletin, *Saudi Arabias Oil Industry: On Course for the 21st century,* Vienna, 1992.

Royal Danish Embassy, *Vejledning for danske i Saudi Arabia (Guide for Danes in SA),* Riyadh, 1995.

Rugh, William A., *The Arab Press, News Media and Political Process in the Arab World,* Syracuse University Press, New York, 1987.

Said Edward W., *Covering Islam, How the Media and the Experts Determine How We See the Rest of the World,* Pantheon Books, New York, 1981.

Salamé, Ghassan (ed.), *Democracy Without Democrats? The Renewal of Politics in the Muslim World,* I.B. Tauris, London, 1995.

Sclove, Richard E., *Democracy and Technology,* The Guildford Press, New York and London, 1995.

Siddiq, Mohammed H., 'He Does Not Play Fair', Lincoln, Nebr., 1990.

Siddiq, Mohammed H., 'A Victim of Ignorant and Greedy Masters', Lincoln Nebraska, 1989.

Siddiq, Mohammed H., 'Saudi Arabia, a country under arrest', Lincoln, Nebraska, 1991

Siddiq, Mohammed H., 'The Prince Ails My Country, He Does Not Play Fair', Lincoln Nebraska, 1989.

Siddiq, Mohammed, 'Why the Boom Went Bust, An Analysis of the Saudi Government', Lincoln Nebraska, USA 1995.

Tamimi, Azzam (ed.), 'Power-Sharing Islam', London, 1993.

Tawfik, Heidi, *Saudi Arabia, A Personal Experience*, Windmill Publishing Company, San José, Calif., 1991.

United Nations, *United Nations and Human Rights, 1945–1995*, New York, 1995.

United Nations, *Human Rights, A Compilation of International Instruments*, New York and Geneva, 1994.

United Nations, *The United Nations and the Iraq-Kuwait Conflict, 1990–1996*, New York, 1996.

U.S. Department of State, Bureau of Consular Affairs, *Consular Information Sheet: Saudi Arabia*, Washington, 1994.

VO, Xuan Han, *Oil, the Persian Gulf States, and the United States*, Praeger, London, 1994.

Weisenborn, Ray E., *Media in the Midst of War, The Gulf War from Cairo to the Global Village*, Adham Center Press, Cairo, 1992.

World Bank, *From Scarcity to Security, Averting a Water Crisis in the Middle East and North Africa*, Washington, 1996.

Yergin, Daniel, *The Prize, The Epic Quest for Oil, Money and Power*, Simon and Schuster, London, 1991.

Addresses

American Islamic Group, P.O.Box 711660, San Diego, California 92171-1660, USA, Tel/Fax (619) 268-8189

Amnesty International, 1 Easton Street, London WC1X 8DJ, United Kingdom, Tel +44 171 413 5500, Fax +44 171 956 1157

Article 19, Lancaster House, 33 Islington High Street, London N1 9LH, United Kingdom, Tel +44 171 278 9292, Fax +44 171 713 1356

The Committee for the Defence of Legitimate Rights, BM Box: CDLR, London WC1N 3XX, United Kingdom

Egyptian Organization for Human Rights, 8/10 Matahaf El-Manyal Street, Manyal er-Rhoda, Cairo, Egypt, Fax (2) 362 1613

Canadian Centre, International PEN, Suite 309, 24 Ryerson Avenue, Toronto, Ontario M5T 2P3, Tel (416) 860 1448

Crescent International, 300 Steelcase Road West, Unit 8, Markham. Ontario Canada L3R 2W2, Tel (905) 474-9292, Fax (905) 474-9293

Human Rights Watch, 1522 K Street NW, Washington, DC 20005-1202 USA

Index on Censorship, Lancaster House, 33 Islington High Street, London N1 9LH, United Kingdom, Tel +44 171 278 2313

Lawyers Committee for Human Rights, 330 Seventh Avenue, 10th Floor, New York, NY 10001, USA, Tel (212) 629 6170, Fax (212) 967 0916

Minnesota advocates for Human Rights, 400 Second Avenue South, Suite 1050, Minneapolis, Minnesota 55401, USA, Tel (612) 341 3302, Fax (612) 341 2971

Redress, 6 Queen Square, London WC1N 3AR, UK

Royal United Services for Defence Studies, Whitehall, London SW1A 2ET, United Kingdom, Tel +44 171 930 5854, Fax +44 171 321 0943

United Nations High Commissioner for Human Rights, Palais des Nations, 1211 Geneve 10, Schwitzerland, Tel +41 22 917 3134, Fax +41 22 917 02 45

The Washington Institute for Near East Policy, 1828 L Street, NW, Suite 1050, Washington, D.C. 20036, USA

On the World Wide Web

Amnesty International:
        http://www.amnesty.org

Arab Net:
        http://www/arab.net

Arab News:
        http://www.arab.net/arabnews/

CACSA (Committee Against Corruption in Saudi Arabia):
        http://www.saudhouse.com

EOHR (Egyptian Organisation for Human Rights):
        http://www.eohr.org.eg

Index on Censorship:
        http://www.oneworld.org/index_oc/

Human Rights Watch/Middle East:
        http://www.saudhouse.com/hrights/watch.html

Lawyers Committee for Human Rights:
http://www.Ichr.org

Minnesota Advocates for Human Rights:
http:/www.umn.edu/humanrts/mnadvocates

Royal Embassay of Saudi Arabia, Washington D.C.:
http://imedl.saudi.net/

State Department:
http://www.state.gov

UN Human Rights:
http://www.un.org/rights/

US House of Representatives/Internet Law Library:
http//law.house.gov/184.html

Saudi Arabian Web Sites:
http://www.liii.com/~hajeri/saudi.html

Maps and Statistics

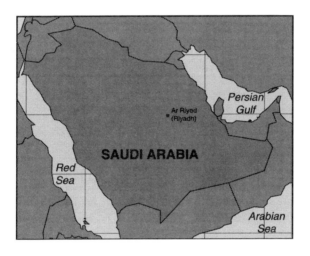

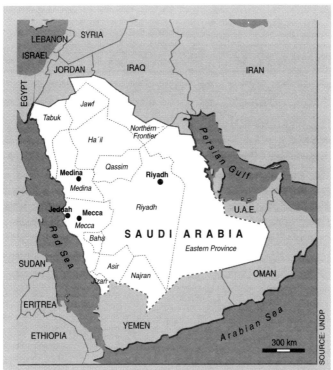

SOURCE: UNDP

Saudi Arabia

Population (millions)	17.1
Land area (thousand hectares)	214,969
GDP (US$ billions), 1993	121.5
Population	
Annual growth rate (%) 1960-1993	4.4
Population doubling rate	2015
(at current growth rate)	2015
Urban population (as of total), 1993	79
Annual urban growth rate (%), 1986 - 93	7.6
Infant mortality rate	
1960	170
1993	28

Human development	
Population (%) with acces to	
...health	97
...safe water, 1975-80	64
...safe water, 1990-95	95
...sanitation, 1990-95	86
Daily calorie supply	
per capita, 1992	2,751

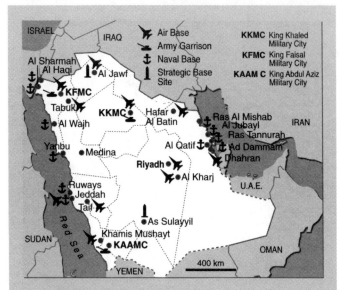

Armed Forces of Saudi Arabia

Army: 70.000 regular troops

- The force has grown from 40.000 before the Gulf War to 60.000 after the war. The current force structure according to 'Janes Intelligence Review' (November 1994) would require around 100.000 to be fully manned, but the authorities 'have faced difficulties in recruiting the necessary personel, especially in technical roles'.

National Guard: 77.000, of which 57.000 active regulars, 20.000 tribal levies

- Consists of tribal volunteers; according to 'Janes Intelligence Review' (November 1994) it serves as 'a counterweight to the regular army and a balance to the Sudairy brothers, who control the throne and the military establishment.' The guard has been used to quell internal unrest in the Eastern Province, but apprantly is building up a conventional army structure.

Air Force: 18.000 regular

- Has developed intensely into the best, most modern Saudi Defence force due to massive investments. Performed surprisingly well during Gulf War along its Western cooperation partners. Only Saudi force believed to be able to cover all national territory.

Navy: 13.500 regular

- Based at Jubail and Jeddah, it serves to secure the Red Coast and the Gulf. Due to lack of manpower, ships and aircraft, it remains highly dependent on foreign navies, i.e. American or British and French forces.

Foreign forces: France 130, US 5.000, UK 200 plus 1 infantry Brigade fom GCC states.

Source of numbers: IISS, London, 1997

Capital punishment

The number of beheadings has been rising in Saudi Arabia.
This is how executions are carried out:

■ The convict usually
is brought to the city
square in front of the
mosque

■ The convict is forced
to kneel with his hands
cuffed on his back

■ The executioner
often has to use several
strikes to separate head
from body

Roots

Death penalty by beheading
originates in tradition and Islam.
It is used as punishment for
offenses like drugs smuggling,
rape, murder, apostacy.

The Koran

'Therefore when we meet the
enemy in fight, smite at their
necks...'
- Sura 47 Mohammed verse 4

Countries with public beheadings on the Arab Peninsula

The Brain

According to Dr. Jacob Mertz/The
Danish section of Amnesty
International, the human brain has
sufficient oxygen stored to persist
about seven seconds after
beheading

Beheadings in Saudi Arabia

Unofficial
statistics of
beheadings:

		192
	85	
54		
1993	1994	1995

Economic indicators

	Saudi Arabia	Arab states	Developing countries
GDP total (US$ billions), 1993	121.5	323	3,780
GDP per capita (1987 US$), 1993		1,298	769
average annual rate of change, 1980-93	-4.5	-5,4	1.0
Foreign direct net investment US $ millions, 1993	-79	1,280	55,420
Gross domestic investment (as % of GDP), 1993	24	24	26
Gross domestic savings (as % of GDP), 1993	27	23	26
Average annual rate of inflation, 1993	-	9.2	289.3

Health

	Saudi Arabia	Arab states	Developing countries
Total fertility rate, 1992	6.4	4.9	3.5
Contraceptive prevalence rate, any method (%), 1986-93	-	34	65
Pregnant Women aged 15 - 49 with anaemia (%), 1975-91	23	-	-
Births attended by trained health personal (%), 1983-94	90	46	63
Maternal mortality rate (per 100,000 live births), 1993	130	392	384
Under five mortality rate (per 1,000 live births), 1994	36	73	97
AIDS cases (per 100,000 people), 1994	0.2	0.5	6.7

Education

	Saudi Arabia	Arab states	Developing countries
Net enrolment ratio (%)			
Primary school			
... Female	57	78	84
... Male	65	89	91
Secondary School	30	44	33
... Female	38	53	39
... Male			
Tertiary students per 100,000 people			
... Female	1,215	925	365
... Male	1,092	1,435	768

Oil Statistics, 1994

	Proven reserves		Production*		Reserves/
	Barrels (bn)	% World share	Barrels/day (m)	% World share	production years
Saudi Arabia	**261.2**	**25.9**	**8.97**	**13.3**	**83.6**
Iraq	100.0	9.9	0.50	0.8	100.0
Kuwait	96.5	9.6	2.09	3.2	100.0
Abu Dhabi	02.2	9.1	2.07	2.9	100.0
Iran	89.3	8.8	3.60	5.5	68.5
Venezuela	64.5	6.4	2.68	4.3	65.4
Mexico	50.8	5.0	3.27	5.0	45.5
Russia	49.0	4.9	6.39	9.9	21.3
USA	30.2	3.0	8.36	12.0	9.8
China	24.0	2.4	2.91	4.5	22.6
OPEC	770.3	76.3	27.30	40.9	79.5

*Includes crude oil, shale oil, oil sands and natural gas liquids

Source: British Petroleum, Statistical Review of World Energi/The Economist Intelligence Unit 1996